Knowledge and Wisdom

Step into the quietness; step into your power. Enter the silence – become aware. Listen within the silence and you will become abundant, the abundance that comes through harmony. The harmony ray is impinging upon the consciousness of humanity. Focussing upon this conflict, it is clear what humanity is in conflict with, and so is the individual - the conflict within the mental and emotional state of being. In silence there is truth; in silence there are no opinions, no control. Can you engage with people whilst being in the silence?

We have worked with the silence in meditation. Can you work with it during the day? The lower mind is the slayer of the real. It is the major problem for achieving harmony, and through harmony there is creativity. If you are familiar with the Fourth Ray of Harmony, you will know it relates to the artist and the poet – all forms of creativity. This comes from an active engagement with the higher mind – creative thinking, abundant thinking.

Turn the environment into a place of learning, don't just exist within it. Does the environment display consciousness? As you look out, can you see harmony? As you look in, can you feel knowing? As you look out, can you see the higher mind in action? As you look in, does the higher mind influence your thinking? Circumscribe an opinion with the higher mind and you will find how useless it is in relationship with harmony. An opinion is different from an observation. Ponder upon the difference. With an opinion, there will be others who will have a different opinion to yours. Both relate to how you think and feel about something, but an observation has no personality identification. The more opinions you have, then the more you will be in conflict with yourself and others and, of course, an opinion carries energy and a forceful negative energy instantly creates conflict.

Relate this now to a belief, then a belief pattern, then give consideration to control. A belief pattern knows itself to be right and anything contrary is wrong. You have no chance against a strong belief pattern, and you will find this everywhere. You may even have one yourself.

In stillness there are no belief patterns. Unconscious repetition of opinion and circumstance creates more opinions based upon them. Go into nature. Have you an opinion on nature, or can you just let nature bring you into harmony? Have you a negative opinion on nature? Nature looks after itself. Can you look after your own nature and what it is based upon? All things are connected; everything affects everything else. Through humanity, thoughts and feelings, the glamour and illusion, will affect everything. Come into your own self-realisation and you will find opinions are but a form of glamour and illusion, and they have no substance. All they do is perpetuate the separation that exists.

Peel away your opinions, retract away from the glamour and illusion of the world; concern yourself with a conscious soul development, become not a judge and jury over life and other people you are taking you away from yourself. Refine your *'I'* identity to become self-conscious. Self-consciousness is the platform for a group conscious, an expression from self to soul and from soul to self, and you will then do without doing. You cannot reach the soul from a place of identification with glamour and illusion, from the thralls of materialism. In fact, soul comes to you. Refine your identity and the soul will come to you.

Carry not many things in your consciousness. Discover yourself – disentangle what is real and unreal. Take your thoughts – what are they based upon? My brother, what do you think about? Do you try to discover us in the spiritual worlds? Do you seek the light, or is your focus upon environment, issues that do not concern you? Humanity does not create its destiny – its destiny is foretold. It just keeps delaying it through its misconceived identifications - too many complications in the name of progress. How does that reflect in your life, in your mind? How does that affect your feelings? You carry many burdens upon your mind as to who you are. Days go by and you are not fulfilled. You have not lived those days – you have just existed. Your circumstance does not stop you expanding your mind. New experiences will occur through your ability to express what you have discovered. Stay within your sorrows and nothing will change.

© Andrew Carter July 2023

See things through different eyes, and many things will not then bother you. Can you imagine the freedom that will give you? You wish to be free, but your understanding of freedom is misplaced. It is not what you believe it to be – in fact, it is yet another prison, because, to you, freedom is being able to do, and go, and own what you want to make your life full of pleasure. In short, freedom, to many, requires money to achieve that freedom they so desire, the never-ending struggle for many to achieve freedom, comfort, and security. Can you imagine the consequences of this identification? And if it is achieved, because you are so used to striving towards it, you will have nothing to strive towards, and at some point, you will feel shallow.

An identification upon money does not give you money. It gives you a duality of money – you will receive it and then it is taken away leading to a dissatisfaction. Maybe even sorrow and anger, and yet this is all part of your identification, especially if you are on the path. In fact, more so, as that identification has to be moved to a soul level of experience to understand what is going on. How much does money control your life and freedom? Money is an aspect to be understood to achieve freedom. Move your identification to the positive aspect of money and what it can do for your spiritual journey and the helping of others. Consideration has to be given to money, and often, if you have a positive identification with money, it will come to you in many mysterious ways.

Yet, my brother, all is not lost because as time goes by, one encounter after another, there comes a point when there will be nowhere to do. Your ego will have lost interest as it will have nothing to control. You will have reached a crisis, a point of tension within the life of the soul. That is when, in that moment of letting go because there is nowhere to go, the light of the soul will come down. The barrier is down, the mind has lost the will of the ego, and there will occur a light-bulb moment, a revelation, giving a realisation of what is occurring. There may be a chance encounter and you will start to turn things into the positive, and the prison will weaken its hold over you. Then you will look around through the eyes of the soul and want to transform your belief patterns to lift your consciousness out of the glamour and illusion. You will start to work towards freedom; you will start to understand freedom from mind and emotions.

© Andrew Carter July 2023

Many will say, *"I am free from emotions. I do not go there. I am intelligent and my intelligence frees me from emotions. I have them under control."* I ask that you ponder upon what has just been said. Read it three times slowly from a state that you will come to know – that is of the soul. Recognition of the soul is through silence, a total pause of everything, a recognition of the space. Through this, your aura will contain silence, your mind will contain a silence yet the light of the soul will become brighter, so action what has been said, and read it once more. Then you will realise that statement indicates the person is *not* free. Their mind is controlling their emotions. They have become a solid citizen within the intelligence of humanity. As a result, many things will be lacking as the emotions equate to feelings, so that intelligent person who is a solid citizen will have little or no feelings. Again, we see a duality, just the same as with money. There are positive feelings, and negative feelings that are disruptive and create problems.

What are those positive feelings that the intelligent person will be lacking? I give you one word – *compassion*, and also the word *love*. Both of these words, which contain certain energies, are non-separative. They are words of caring. Feelings relate to a caring nature, a compassionate understanding. Love will relate understanding to intelligence, but not the intelligence I am speaking about, which can be classified as intellect. Yes, even a very high intellect still relates to the lower intelligence unless it possesses compassion and love, which comes from the soul, from the heart. I am talking about the higher intelligence, which does not relate to intellect or knowledge of an intellectual nature. Once more we see a duality with the word *love*. There is no duality with the word *compassion*, so there is negative love and positive love. Yes, positive love can be present within a relationship if compassion and caring exists, but there is the negative love of desire to be fulfilled in a sexual way, and that can create a lot of problems.

Previously, you were asked to ponder upon the word *control*. Let me use that word *'the desire to control for selfish ends.'* Control only lasts so long as it comes from the lower mind. Situations and events will bring that control over love to an end, but regarding love and desire, there is a pattern and a focus of energies within the lower centres of consciousness. I will refer to 'centres', but you will understand them as chakras. Many reading this will have an understanding of chakras and their psychology.

The Ray of Love and Wisdom is in full manifestation and governs the solar system. The earth is governed by intelligence, and that ray of energy consciousness has been in manifestation for hundreds of years, along with the Ray of Science. Note the ray energy is love and wisdom, and the wisdom comes from the higher intelligence. Yes, it is beyond time, not like the lower mind or even intellect. All this is within time, yet from beyond time you can be inspired by the higher intelligence that also carries love and wisdom, which leads to heart thinking. Think of this as being soul, heart, and mind in resonance. The mind is then influenced by the soul and heart, so it thinks beyond intellect, beyond knowledge that is already written, beyond facts. Knowledge, as it exists, will change.

Seek the higher knowledge for the future. Past knowledge can be useful, but only see it as that. Go beyond time and there does exist the overshadowing wisdom. It contains the future wisdom, also past wisdom, but the past wisdom will be what is useful for the future wisdom. Stay not in the past. The harmony ray fully manifests in 2025. Remember its creativity, its negative aspects as it enters into duality upon the physical plane and everything that comes beyond time when it enters time, because a duality is conflict, so it is Harmony through Conflict. Already you can see where this conflict may come from. You may view the conflict aspects of the Ray of Harmony as being the negative aspects as it can create conflict within your personality, but that conflict will only happen if there are aspects of your personality that may not be in harmony, so it is a positive aspect of the Ray of Harmony and also a negative aspect concerning the personality. As it produces discomfort it will challenge the intellect; it will challenge behaviour; it will bring things to the surface to be transmuted and transformed. So, the advents of the Fourth Ray can feel uncomfortable, but in the light of the soul, that one conflict produces revelations, a clarity of mind, and yet another step towards freedom.

Systemic energies are Second Ray energies. I once more present the two aspects – Love and Wisdom. This is what humanity seeks to achieve for its evolution, and that refers to every individual human being, including yourself. So, ponder upon love and

© Andrew Carter July 2023

wisdom in relationship to yourself. Take love away from the personality identification to a soul identification, then bring it back to the personality. Wisdom is something most people can relate to a wise man or woman who speaks words of profound importance. I mentioned the overshadowing cloud of wisdom, so after you have brought love back to the personality, seek the overshadowing cloud of wisdom. This is a heart approach. The higher mind them impresses the lower mind in many abstract ways, not just of a spiritual nature, as everything corresponds. Wisdom is not just of a spiritual nature, or to put it in a better way, it comes from the vast library beyond time, from the heart love and the higher mind impressing the lower mind. It reaches down into everyday life and affairs, hence you will be receiving wisdom and expressing wisdom through your everyday life experience. Because it is a natural process, it requires no mental approach, no control of any sort of process. You will, at first, not realise you are doing it. Subtle changes will happen and they will go unnoticed. Even as time goes by, you may not notice the difference in yourself. Many have this potential for change but have no idea of the process, and think that through mantras, seeking higher worlds, angels – all sorts of things – that they will rise into the higher spiritual height of ascension. Yes, it is good to seek those things, but if your mind is full of environment and all those things mentioned, then there is no space for the wisdom, no opportunity to relinquish all those things that hold you a prisoner of the planet. They just create another prison.

You have broken out of the prison that concerns many. The next is the prison of control. The powerhouse of control is the solar plexus - in relationship to that is the ego. We watch in sadness to see what the lack of control gives to you – fear, uncertainty, discomfort. You try to keep things the same as you are familiar with them, and any change can cause a problem unless, through your control, you cause it to happen. Notice the work *cause.* I add the word *effect.* How do you react if things are out of your control? Suddenly, your emotional nature gives you a problem, combined with a negative thought pattern over which you have no control, you become distressed and seek to find the answer to give you back control. Once in control again, you can relax back into the world you have created through your control.

© Andrew Carter July 2023

Knowledge and Wisdom

Have you started to realise all this creates effect? The effects of your lack of control you try to overcome, but in doing so, you create other effects and what are the effects of your control in the first place, as control involves others, it involves your life circumstances. So, you are giving others no freedom along with your own lack of freedom. If you have control over something, think about the stress and tension it causes you to maintain that control. There is a possibility you have no realisation that you are controlling and projecting outward to others. You may say they are trying to control you, or giving you a problem.

Where does this control come from? I have mentioned the solar plexus. It will come from an over-active solar plexus. The planet Mars is related to the solar plexus, and is a major influence for the personality that functions from the lower centres and are of a materialistic nature. That influence loses its power as the prison door starts to open, and another planetary influence affects the solar plexus – Mars gives way to Neptune, the energy of devotion.

I must state there are seven sacred planets in the solar system. Neptune is a sacred planet and from Neptune comes the energies of devotion - not from the planet itself, but via the planet from the sun. Mars is not a sacred planet (just the same as Earth), but all is evolving. The energies of devotion are waning as the energies of magic and manifestation are increasing in frequency, just the same as the harmony ray. As far as control is concerned, seek the harmony ray to bring yourself into harmony. Your identification is the planet Mercury. Also seek the ray of love and wisdom. They are both upon the same line. Bring them into the heart via your identification with the planets, from the soul to the heart chakra, then drag them down into the solar plexus.

I am taking this beyond the planetary ring-pass-not into a solar identification. Your chakras (or, as I like to call them, *centres of consciousness*) have a relationship with the planets of the solar system.

You are part of the greater whole. It is wise to encompass that within your thinking, and because you are part of the greater whole, then you will seek the freedom that the greater whole can give you. And relinquish control. Bring the greater whole into your consciousness, feel yourself a part of its awesome magnitude. A very simple thing to do, if you can go into the silence and become aware of the silence of the space. You can, if you wish, then ponder upon money and control. I suggest not initially, as you need to form an identification and relationship with the greater whole. Your intellectual mind will ask as this point what the greater whole is, because it has not the capacity to understand the concept. If you follow what I have said, you will start to realise what it is, because it will be impressing you in many ways. It is worth recording your experiences, even though you cannot understand them.

Understanding is something you continue to want to gain. You cannot understand from your surface mind, or the mind that wants to understand. Once more, you will be within your prison of understanding. You are within time, and impressions from the greater whole, although that incorporates what lies within time, comes from beyond time, so the understanding is not an instant thing. Even if you lift yourself to the higher mind (which is also beyond time), there could be a time delay regarding understanding. The higher mind impresses the lower mind with the concepts of the greater whole, but the lower mind has to be in a condition to receive what the higher mind is saying. Remember, the higher mind can be abstract. This is very annoying for the lower mind, as it wants to understand, but it wants to understand now, instantly! That is not how it works. Yes, sometimes there can be an instant revelation, but you see, when you break out of all the prisons, there are no set boundaries between one thing and another. That is what you have to realise – everything connects to everything else. Once you have that realisation by experience, you will also realise there are no coincidences.

If you are wanting to understand constantly, and this can happen once upon the path, then you have created a prison. Realise that what you have that you seek to understand will go into your sub-conscious and eventually will come into the surface mind, but you have to allow it to do so. You think from intellect and if you cannot remember something, you think you have not gained from it because you could not remember it or understand it, yet as times goes on, what you experience will give you the understanding of what you could not remember. It will stimulate what has gone into the sub-conscious. If you seek to control your mind by listening with the objective to intellectually understand, then you may well become drained and get a headache. You will stop the flow of energy through the head centres of consciousness.

© Andrew Carter July 2023

Now, there are others, when they don't understand, who just ignore what is being projected as they are not prepared to give consideration to any concepts that go beyond their level of understanding. They will not seek to know. It's a complete shutdown. The brain consciousness has been programmed to do that, and what seeks to do that? The significance of this is a controlling nature, an inflexibility of mind – the concrete mind. I mention in relationship with this, the Fifth Ray of Concrete Science, which comes to us via the planet Venus. The planet Earth has a strong relationship with it – it is said that the earth planetary Logos come from Venus. This ray is a ray of attribute, therefore we see a duality here – concrete science, then science and discovery. This ray has been highly active, playing upon the consciousness of humanity. This you can quite easily understand, but now it is starting the recede, making way for the harmony ray.

One last statement upon the activity between Venus and the Earth. There is a meditating group between the two called *The Reflecting Lights.* Also looking over the earth is a perfected being known as the *Silent Watcher.* The Reflecting Lights are a linking group between Earth and Venus. You are probably unaware of these identifications, and although I have given no information on them or the Silent Watcher, you can ponder upon them. How do they relate to the evolution of the earth and earth's humanity? What energies do the Masters receive from them?

Now, control can only last so long. Many factors will play out upon a controlling force until, eventually, the control is broken in one way or another. Related to control is cause and effect. Related to understanding is consciousness, related to both is the Law of Karma.

The Third Ray of Intelligence comes to us via the planet Saturn, but the planet Saturn is also the planet of Karma. In relationship to the Tree of Life we see the Sephiroth Geburah, so understanding can come from seven planets of the solar system and the ten sephiroth of the Tree of Life. Understanding comes from Jupiter (wisdom) and gives the power to discriminate. Through negativity, you are not discriminating with understanding. You will have an aspect of control and very strong opinions.

© Andrew Carter July 2023

Karma redresses the balance, so control can come under the Law of Karma as control wields the energy of force. There is a difference between force and energy. Energy is of a healing and spiritual nature; force is what is applies upon the physical planes and is an aspect of control. Another aspect is a lack of understanding. Force suppresses understanding; it closes off the head centres which are receptive to energy and the inspiration from the soul. This is what is applied upon the physical plane and is an aspect of control and a lack of understanding.

My brother, you have to discriminate yourself. Do you hold your life together through force or energy? Consider force in connection with its effects upon the chakras and aura, and the results of those effects. Now consider energy and its effects upon the chakras and aura. Energy is more subtle in its effects. Force is powerful, and the more focus and identification that force has, the more powerful it becomes on a physical level. The soul produces energy and can transmute force within the lower centres which relate to the energy of soul as being light. We know the light of the soul contains and transmits the three major rays of aspect, so you can consider those three streams of energy when bringing down from the soul its light.

I give you the tree rays of aspect:

Ray One	Will and Purpose (power), Divine Will.	Red	Vulcan
Ray Two	Love and Wisdom, Divine Will .	Blue	Jupiter
Ray Three	Active Intelligence, Divine Intelligence	Yellow	Saturn

You can do a transference of mind to soul, soul to mind, but first initiate a heart-soul alignment. Once a flow of energy is created, bring that light down through your centres of consciousness. You can then select a specific energy. Be inspired because if you notice, I have given the planets these energies flow through. Bear in mind, they flow *through* the planet and are not *from* the planet. Now, with this you can transmute the effects of Mars upon the solar plexus. These effects you will be experiencing through cause and a relativity to Karma, so you will be under the influence also of the planet Saturn – not what passes through Saturn (which you can see is Active Intelligence and Divine Intelligence), but the karmic consequences of Saturn once more loses its power, then things change and the influence will be

Divine Intelligence, which will overcome Karma and create positive effects from causes of good will.

Three things to consider: Right Relationships, Harmlessness and Right Speech. The Lords of Karma are known as the Lipika Lords. Now, Karma can be related to past life, or the consequences of past life being adjusted in this life. It is not as simple as that, and even if, to some degree, you could read the Akashic Records, you would fail to see the truth. It is best not to engage with past life – only with an advanced disciple. It is *this* life that is important to man, and the future. You can, in one year, advance in consciousness, by analogy, thirty years, or even the equivalent of an entire lifetime. This is the opportunity that is available, but you have to give over yourself to doing it, and also take the opportunities for your spiritual growth. When you do, transformation will occur, and the rapidity of your growth may present to you the chance to relinquish certain personality traits that are in opposition to your spiritual growth.

Keep a sense of humour, my brother. Do not sink into negativity or over-sensitivity, as that could be your downfall, and you will find yourself back in the personality and susceptible to glamour and illusion. Revelation will come, but do not criticise what that revelation reveals to you. Remember Right Relations. Consider what that means. It is more than what it emotionally appears to be – it is not about being nice. It is being aware of what you can cause through Wrong Relations. You do not wish to do that, so sometimes you need to think about things. The transference of consciousness from the soul will allow you to do that. In fact, the transference will become automatic as time goes by, and will require no effort on your part. You will have created the channel and activated the motion from mind to soul, soul to mind, so your thinking will be from the soul.

Always remember, never give your identity away – who you are. Allow yourself to naturally expand who you are. Your thinking of what it is to be spiritual is outdated today. It is required for you to be active within one's environment; that is who you are; that is your mission as a member of the Hierarchy – a disciple. I use that word not with a religious context. So, your spiritual expression will be according to your environment, and will be projected by your personality, the creativity of your

© Andrew Carter July 2023

personality which is unique to you. Do not lose who you are – use who you are. The man, the soul, comes down into your everyday life.

Another light will appear in the solar plexus, so there will be two lights. One the personality, and the other the soul and they will work together in your expression the corresponding higher chakras to the solar plexus (the throat) and via the throat you will relay truth. You may not be popular at times, but truth will be very hard for you not to express.

I give you more information. A centre will develop between the heart and throat chakras, up the spine. This centre will be a transferring centre from the heart to the higher chakras to the soul, creating an expansion of consciousness and awareness via the higher heart, as such, located in the centre of the crown chakra. In fact, all the centres have an energy identification with the crown chakra. From this, you can see the importance of the crown chakra, and, of course, the pineal gland will activate. It will produce a tiny point of light, lighting the brain consciousness.

Ponder upon what has been said. Read through it slowly, meditate upon it and create the inter-connections. When you look at the psychology of the head centre, it is widely known as acceptance. This has to be taken to the soul to fully understand the meaning, as a personality identification with acceptance can create a passive state based upon the aspect of love with no will or intelligence involved. The will and intelligence will be of a lower nature and will suppress until such a time when it will surface through the solar plexus and the brow, creating a complete reversal of what has been accepted, so acceptance has to come from the soul. A much-preferred word is *understanding*, and that covers all the aspects of the other centres of consciousness. Understand from the many levels of experience, and that understanding will be reflected in the correspondences of the other chakras that lie within the crown centre.

Again, understanding comes from the soul, which not only carries love, but also the will and intelligence, and that will be carried forth into right relations. You will find that what is required for that is discrimination. Can you initiate right relations within your life? It is not difficult if you are free from glamour and illusion. This is a natural process through the embodiment of the soul and, of course, related to that is the word *freedom*, so you have understanding, discrimination and freedom. You have to understand to be able to discriminate what is real and unreal, or what is glamour and illusion, or truth.

Ponder upon understanding in relationship to what has been said. Also, give consideration to discrimination. You can be free from glamour and illusion if you have the power of recognition. How do you recognise? By stepping back in the light of the soul, that great revealing light that will open your eyes to what is happening. You will understand what is happening through detachment, specifically to outcomes. Two aspects to meditate upon here are *open your eyes* and *detachment to outcomes.* Regarding the eyes, you see what you think and feel. This is in relationship to your personality, also glamour and illusion.

Let us relate all this to the three aspects of the sun, but first, consider that the energies, or rays, I have been referring to which come via the planets, tracking back, then going to the sun, then the planets, then to Earth. Obviously, I am making an earth identification, but these energies criss-cross throughout the solar system, manifesting cyclically for a certain period of time upon a planet – for example, Earth. They are cyclic upon the other planets of the solar system, but the heart of the solar system and the life-force of the solar system, is the sun, which has three aspects, three different types of energy.

Fire by friction	physical sun	personality
Solar fire	heart of sun	soul
Electric fire	central spiritual sun	Monad

You can see I have related the three aspects of a human being to the three aspects of the sun. In relationship to fire by friction is the planet Mars, which is the controlling force of the solar plexus, so you can see that fire by friction is related to glamour and illusion - all that I have spoken about before many times, opinions, etc. Also, the friction that is created forms a point of tension, which leads to a relinquishment of certain characteristics of the personality that is in friction. Can you see also a connection with the Fourth Ray of Harmony through Conflict.

© Andrew Carter July 2023

Knowledge and Wisdom

The conflict and the friction are not to be avoided. They are there to create growth – spiritual growth, self-consciousness, an awareness that you think are not there. The heart of the sun-soul relates to understanding. It creates a heart opening, a consciousness based upon love and wisdom – heart thinking. Here there is a relationship with the Second Ray of Love and Wisdom. I have related the Fourth Ray to fire by friction. Consider this comes via the planet Mercury, which is related to the intuition – the Winger Messenger.

A lot to think about. Read through this work initially without trying to understand it or memorise it. Then you can go back for a greater understanding, and certain aspects of the work will leap out at you to ponder upon and expand upon for your own understanding, and also for others. This is Right Relations with all the parts of the whole – nothing is separate – so form these relations with the whole through identification, that's all you have to do. The rest will happen – you don't have to strive for it to happen.

What is required to create harmony is intelligence. The third aspect, Divine Intelligence, overcomes fire by friction, which keeps things apart. Can you think of where in your life fire by friction occurs whereby you keep things apart? Obviously through discrimination we choose what we engage in. That is not keeping things apart. If your consciousness criticises that which you are discriminating, that is separation as discrimination relates to the heart of the sun, then you are not keeping things apart in your consciousness as you see what you are discriminating as part of the whole. This is the secret – to be a part of the whole on many levels which you will expand into, realising the interconnectivity of everything that exists, whether in physical form, or the many forms beyond the physical. Hence, you will not be a prisoner of the planet.

The central spiritual sun - electric fire – is the Divine Will that blends with the Divine Love of the heart of the sun. You can imagine the sun in your mind and if you align heart and soul, create a transference of consciousness soul-mind, mind-soul, then the sun identifies with the heart of the sun, then the central spiritual sun. Have no expectation – just be within the silence and the spiritual space. Results will come later.

© Andrew Carter July 2023

Knowledge and Wisdom

I have mentioned the eyes. The right eye relates to the crown and the Atmic Plane (will). The left eye relates to the brow and the Buddhic plane (love). The Third Eye between the eyebrows is the eye of the soul, etheric in nature. Through all that is being presented, you will be developing etheric consciousness to see and understand beyond the physical. Focusing your identification with the chakras is already doing that, and your understanding of the etheric body as it interpregnates the physical also increases your understanding of etheric consciousness. So, you can look out upon the world through the physical eyes. I have mentioned you see what you think and feel. I have just presented the spiritual connection to the physical eyes, and that will form a triangle with the third eye of the soul, so what you see will be through the aspects of Divine Love, Will and Intelligence. That has to be interpreted by the brain consciousness, which may not be in line with the divine aspects as it has retained memory. This is where the conflict can occur. Eventually the brain consciousness will release what is holding it back from the expansion of consciousness the divine aspects will bring, so keep viewing life from these divine aspects and the soul, and do not be disturbed if negative memory surfaces.

Your etheric body, which can be viewed in the appropriate light, is just outside of the skin. We classify it as the etheric physical body because your etheric body underlies every part of your body, so there is an etheric liver, etheric spleen, etc. Also, an etheric leg, which explained to you why people who have lost their leg can still feel the leg. The etheric and the physical and so intertwined that when the physical is no more, the etheric body disappears back into etheric substance, and the person finds themself living their life in their astral body.

The point I am coming to is that the etheric body surrounds the brain and also there is an astral and mental sheath that surrounds the brain. Now, if you relate that to what has been said about the eyes, and about many opinions, etc., you can see why a duality will exist between what you see and what you think about and feel. You will be reviewing the situation that has been presented twice more, which are: you see what you think and feel. You will start to think and feel from the soul and its divine aspects and the sheath surrounding the brain will become positive to those aspects. This will be via your three head centres, which form another triangle as they all have become magnetic to those divine aspects.

© Andrew Carter July 2023

Consider that the high aspects of the astral body relate to joy, so you will develop a sense of humour, you will become more creative with your expression, and many other things concerning creativity. Your mind will suddenly have space as it will not be thinking all those things related to glamour and illusion. Its focus will not be the ego, who likes to talk about itself. All will be revealed as you look out through the eyes from the soul, so your focus is upon the soul, which gives understanding. Do not submerge yourself in your problems as you will be reviewing your problems from a thinking and feeling aspect that has the problems, so it all just runs around. In fact, it could get worse. When the soul comes into your thinking and feeling, them the problem lessens in its intensity, until there is no problem.

So, at this point, make an identification through the imagination with what I am about to say.

> You have the soul above the head moving through the higher mental. You reach the Buddhic plane of love - your left eye is connecting to this plane.
>
> Above that you have the plane of atmic (will) - your right eye is connected to this plane. Your Third Eye is connected to the soul.
>
> Your head centre (crown) is connected to your right eye and atmic. Your brow is connected to your left eye (Buddhic).
>
> Your alta major centre at the back of your head where the skull meets the neck, sends energy down your spine, passing through the back centres to the base. You may wish to take this down to the earth.
>
> Your soul above your head is connected to you via three threads of light – one to the head chakra, the life thread; one to the throat, the creative thread; and one to the crown, the consciousness thread identifies with each of those threads.
>
> You also have three bodies of light. You have an etheric body of light surrounding you; you have a soul body of light surrounding you halfway into your aura; and on the periphery a monadic body of light.
>
> You can imagine the lights from these bodies flowing through your aura.

> Through a meditative pondering, you have learnt a lot. Just sit with the energy.

I brought in the three threads of light from the soul. Let us consider the creative thread into the throat. This is your expression through sound. Can you be creative through your expression? That will reflect in many ways other than sound. What would stop your creative expression for the soul? A fear of not saying the right thing, of being liked? Many things of a psychological nature – self-worth, lack of power. At some point you will not be able to stop your creative expression, because as you come to understand more, then you will come to know the truth, and your expression will be based upon truth. You will start to see through the eyes and your sense of hearing what in not truth. Can you imagine living in truth? Truth, as it comes into your expanded consciousness, is truth. There is *freedom* and *liberation.* Give those two words (which carry an energy consciousness) a consideration in relationship to the etheric consciousness of the word *truth*.

So, what words would you identify your heart, throat, and crown chakras with, in the light of truth? This is not a self-identification, it is a soul-identification, so just use the space and stillness.

> Identify with the soul then the chakras – the words will drop into your head. These words will also have a relationship to the three threads,

> Now you have those words, you can drop down to the solar plexus, sacral and base, dropping then to the earth centre to give another word.

> To complete this is to move up to the brow chakra. Now you have a set of words in relationship to the chakras. Something to ponder upon. As you know the psychology of the chakras, there will be much to gain.

> Also, take yourself away from yourself to find the universal nature of the words.

© Andrew Carter July 2023

Knowledge and Wisdom

There is a lot you can experiment with here. Words can open doors. They create pathways of consciousness. It's just a matter of expanding the concept of the word. Can you do this, if only for a short period of time? One word will produce many words that will have a plane of identification. You may achieve nothing to start with, but you will be knocking at the door, so to speak, and eventually, probably when you least expect it, something will inspire you. The words will eventually cause that to happen because you have thought about them and they will be committed to your memory. Your memory will bring them into your mind because your memory does that, then the energy consciousness of the word will reveal itself with no effort, so your thinking upon the words requires no effort – something you are not used to. You try without trying – ponder upon those words, then you will come to understand your inter-connectivity to the higher planes of consciousness.

Through not trying, you are becoming receptive. Your vibrations are lifting in frequency as all lower vibrations drop away, then, within that moment in time, you will connect, and the divine consciousness will relay to you, its wisdom. How do you perceive wisdom? Wisdom can come from the most ordinary person who, on perception, has no spiritual identification – but they do. You would not be able to recognise an advanced disciple or a Master of the wisdom. Never judge a book by its cover! When you are on the path, wisdom will come to you in many forms within your physical environment. Wisdom will also come into your mind in quiet moments, or the moments you give over to thinking.

If I said to you that you can possess the wisdom and that you are advanced enough to receive it, can you believe that statement – that you are advanced enough to receive it? Ponder for a moment upon that, and observe yourself from the soul. Have you any negative statements upon your ability to receive and express the wisdom? It comes in many forms. Just imagine the wisdom overshadowing you, the raincloud of knowable things, as expressed by Patanjali a long time ago. We are moving rapidly into a new age, and why is this so? Because the energies coming to the planet are of a different nature to those over the last two thousand years, which had a Sixth Ray dimension – idealism and devotion with a high activity of the Third Ray of Active Intelligence, and the Fifth Ray Concrete Science. The Second Ray of Love and Wisdom is always in manifestation.

© Andrew Carter July 2023

If you ponder upon the meaning of those energies and the history of humanity over the last two thousand years, you will understand the happenings of the times, especially if you understand when the rays slipped down into the physical plane – mental, emotional, and physical - they come into duality. Positive and negative aspects. Rays stimulate consciousness. Humanity's consciousness has been governed by those rays which have produced institutions, laws, patterns of thinking, ways of behaviour, etc. Now the energies are changing, those three rays are receding. Their influence is starting to wane, in particular the Sixth Ray that governed. It has been moving out over the last several hundred years, and is being replaced by the Seventh Ray of Ceremonial Order and Magic, or, what can be called – manifestation.

The Seventh Ray governs the physical plane so expect things to suddenly happen. (Rays?) Three and Five are also losing power to make way for the Fourth Ray of Harmony, but it is known as *harmony through conflict*. The conflict mentioned concerns the personality, which has been influenced by the negative aspects of the Sixth Ray, and the Third (intelligence), and the Fifth (science). We are in a period of transition from one ray to another. The Seventh Ray is so different to the Sixth, magical in the way it works, and the harmony ray stimulates and brings forth the creative arts. This ray is in full manifestation in the year 2025. This is also the year of the 100 Year Conclave of the Masters of Wisdom, when they decide upon their action for the next hundred years. We have to make that transition in consciousness to embody those energies and prepare to bring forth the new and the different. We are moving into an age of enlightenment. Can we grasp this opportunity as we perceive the old trying to hold grip upon control? The control will break as more people lift their consciousness out of the glamour and illusion so prevalent today.

Let us consider Scorpio, a sign of initiation. The myth and legend concerns the nine-headed hydra - each head representing a vice to be overcome. These heads symbolise the appetite associated with sex, comfort, and money. The second three heads the passion of fear, hatred, and desire for power. The third three heads represent the vices of the unilluminated mind, pride, separateness, and cruelty. This was one of the Labours of Hercules – to slay the nine-headed hydra. As he cut off the heads, they grew back again. He was trying to conquer the hydra with physical

© Andrew Carter July 2023

force. He then dropped down to his knees in humility, and picked up the hydra into the light. The hydra could not withstand the light. Remember what the hydra represents, so if you take your mind to the light, the light of the soul, then you too can overcome the aspects of the hydra that influence you. They represent the appetite, passion, and the unilluminated mind. A sane and natural approach is required to these vices, and can only truly be understood from the soul. Most of these vices you have a clear understanding of, and have overcome to a degree. Take the vices of the unilluminated mind:

Pride. Is pride an enemy of yours? Can you be humble? Can you be honest with yourself and others? Can you bow down in humility? Pride is of the ego and won't back down or lose face.

Separateness. Do you view life with likes and dislikes? This relates to what has been written about opinion. It is not separate to observe the separateness of others without judgement or criticism. It is just how it is. Do you alienate yourself? It is wise to discriminate. Do you put everything in a box and have preferences over others? If you believe in the interconnecting of everything, you are not engaging in separateness.

Cruelty. This is easily understood regarding the physical body, but what about mental and emotional cruelty that cannot be so easily seen? At this time, there is much confusion concerning this, as mostly it is related to relationships. Consider the word *control* in this context. Consider also *criticism.* Many people display those aspects, but it when it is constantly and repetitively aimed with force at someone that it becomes cruelty. It bombards the senses and takes away personal power.

Consider also what comes through environment, what you listen to. One of the passions is fear, so whatever generates fear is cruel. Many things do that – be careful what you listen to. There is a wave of fear-mongering that is taking over the mind, and many have perceived this as being so, and their numbers are growing. Shed your authoritarian beliefs, the control of centuries of institutions and rules. Do not believe the fear. Step into truth. Keep your focus upon the soul and not the fear, and it will drop away from you.

© Andrew Carter July 2023

Hatred. You can easily understand. Also consider jealousy to want something that somebody else has. This is so prevalent in relationships. The opposite of hatred is love, so concern yourself not with what others say or do, and do not create jealousy or overwhelming desire for something. Always go from heart to soul and let go of obsession – yet another prison, another box to trap your mind.

The desire for power can relate to money and control. Here the solar plexus is highly active, and the mind fixed upon what it desires. The intellectual mind will activate the desire for power, and focus upon that desire. The ego will become all-powerful. This desire for power and recognition runs through all aspects of life, even within spiritual circles, because of this.

Sex, in itself, is not a vice, but an over-emphasis upon it and its deviants, becomes a vice. A sane approach is required. It is a human function, but it can become perverted, so it is worth reflecting in the light of the soul regarding sex as to what is a human function and what is a distortion of a human function.

Comfort can occupy the attention of many. The phrase *comfort zone* or *I am having a pyjama day,* or something like that, indicates a trend towards a withdrawal from activity, from engaging with life and environment. There is nothing wrong with being comfortable or having nice things, but within comfort there is no expansion of consciousness, no challenge as to activity to engage the soul, no chance to rise above glamour and illusion into the light of the soul. You will delay your destiny and your unique purpose for this life.

So, these are the challenges of Scorpio, but realise there is no separation between the travel through the Zodiac. The challenges of Scorpio are not to be feared. On each full moon there is an opportunity for realisations. What are the thoughts upon the full moon? How do people treat the full moon experience? Firstly, they look for the negative impact of the full moon, just like they do for the negative impact of the planets in the solar system and what that is likely to cause. There is a lot of information out there concerning all this, and that will hold you down upon the ordinary wheel of astrology.

© Andrew Carter July 2023

Attempts are being made to understand the reverse wheel, but referring to the opposite sign as being the full moon, for example, the full moon in Leo – it is being said that it is the full moon in Aquarius, and this is not correct. Aquarius is the opposite sign to Leo and starts to have an influence as you engage with spiritual work and meditation. Its positive aspects will transmute the negative aspect of your sun sign. So, look at your sign for its positive attributes. You may well see they are all having an influence upon you. You then spiral upwards in consciousness via the interplay of your sun sign and your opposite sign, with an influence from your preceding sign and the succeeding sign. You will be moving onto the reverse wheel of astrology, and all the planetary negatives that happen will have no impact upon you, as you will not be influenced by the planets, but by the energies flowing through the aura of the planet – the Seven Rays of Consciousness. Keep your eye upon the soul, not upon any negative impacts of the full moon or planets. The negative does not concern you, as you are a disciple who is going beyond their influence to higher spiritual influence. Believe you are a disciple, because if you were not, you would not be reading this presentation and have got this far through it!

The full moon is an opportunity for insight, developing intuition, and furthering your ashramic connection., Remember, your overshadowing spiritual soul lives within the Ashram. It is when earth, moon and sun are in alignment, and therefore you are also in alignment with the Hierarchy of Masters upon the Buddhic plane and the Ashrams. Can you see, if your focus is upon the negative of what I have mentioned, the opportunity is lost. You will be within your personality, not your soul.

Consider also the evolution of humanity started with the Saturn evolution to the old sun, then the moon chain, finally manifesting physically upon the earth, so we have come from the sun and moon. Look how they govern the earth, and also your own nature. The light with the dark, the seasons and cycles which can also be the seasons and cycles of the soul. Then also ponder upon Saturn – the planet of Karma, where it all began.

Just to reiterate once more, once you start to resonate with the opposite sign, you will become less affected by the negative aspects of your sun sign and the energies from the planets themselves. You will be free from their influence. They will not affect

© Andrew Carter July 2023

you. Take note of this – it is a key to your spiritual growth. The full moon cycles will become a period of opportunity. At the full moon you are in direct alignment with the Hierarchy of Masters. You will also, because of this, be developing your purpose for this life – all else will be but distraction.

There is a lot out there that can be a distraction, so when you have, for example, Mercury in retrograde, or Pluto over the next month, which will cause problems of an emotional nature, it will not apply to you. Also, I must mention here what is called *light body activations and systems*, all due to these planetary or extra-planetary energies. This will not apply to you, and is mostly related to being ungrounded. That statement may surprise you, but this is the illusion. Let me mention what is known as *ascension* - to ascend to a higher plane of consciousness, out of the physical uncertainties, the pain, and the sorrow to ascend to that higher plane, where all is light and love, and you can live eternal within this nirvana. This is not how it is, because those who do live upon those planes have come to know sacrifice. Relate sacrifice to what has been said.

Many people seek this way out of the physical plane through the light body activation. Only you can activate your light body and, and mentioned previously, there are three light bodies of which few people are aware. They are also mantras and other practices, including the raising of the kundalini. There are exercises to do this, but do they understand what they are doing? There are seven major chakras, and between them there is a disc or web separating them. This is not separation as such, but once that disc or web has gone, then all the chakras become one – complete enlightenment. This happens when the kundalini rises from the base, up the spine to the crown, burning away the disc or web separating the chakras. This is a natural process as your consciousness and awareness expands into the higher divine worlds, but many seek to force this process through meditations and exercises. Fortunately, many have not the will to cause this to happen. Now, can you imagine that the kundalini rises because you have reached a point in your spiritual development whereby it will just happen? If you force it to happen when you have not reached that level of consciousness, then it can cause extreme mental and emotional problems, and also insanity.

© Andrew Carter July 2023

Knowledge and Wisdom

A lot can be said about all this. How does it appear to you? Does it appear self-centred requiring a degree of selfishness to seek to escape to a better place? As the Tibetan quotes, *'You will not want it'*. Thought provoking regarding sacrifice. Let me give you the Affirmation of the Disciple for some clarity:

> I am a point of light within a greater light
> I am a strand of loving energy within this stream of love divine
> I am a point of sacrificial fire, focussed within the fiery will of God
> And thus, I stand
>
> I am a way by which men may achieve
> I am a source of strength enabling them to stand
> I am a beam of light shining upon their way
> And thus, I stand
>
> And standing thus, revolve
> And tread this way the ways of men
> And know the ways of God
> And thus, I stand

As you are a disciple, this will have great meaning for you; you may well have knowledge of this affirmation. There are three parts to it. The first part affirms what you are and where you stand - *I am a point of light within a greater light*. You are a point of light because you are aware of the soul, therefore your aura carries the light of the soul which can be seen from the higher planes. You also affirmed that you are a part of a greater light. You have expanded your consciousness into the One Life, and there lies a greater light.

> Now, at this moment, you can take this into your imagination.
>
> Affirm - *I am a point of light within a greater light*. Seek the greater light, then affirm - *I am a strand of loving energy within the stream of divine love*.
>
> Bring that into your imagination, then affirm – *I am a point of sacrificial fire focussed within the fiery will of God*. Bring that into your imagination – you are bringing in love and will.

© Andrew Carter July 2023

Knowledge and Wisdom

Then say – *And thus, I stand.* You will feel the energies of identification, so stay with that for a few minutes.

Now say – *I am a way by which men may achieve.* This is what you have to offer to others. Your way and identification can be relayed to others so they may achieve what you have achieved. Ponder upon that, realising how far you have come to be able to do this.

Then say – *I am a source of strength enabling them to stand.* Your strength lies in the fact that you have overcome glamour and illusion, and can stand within the light, thus displaying a poise and a strength enabling others to stand in their own light by your example. Realise this.

Now say – *I am a beam of light shining upon their way.* Thus, you are revealing the path and the way forward, giving them a purpose and inspiration, and revealing also their qualities.

State – *And thus, I stand.* Spend a few minutes pondering your intuition.

Now affirm that you are revolving upon the pedestal of light and going back towards humanity.

Say – *And standing thus, revolve.* Then – *and tread this way the ways of men* and *know the ways of God.*

Ponder for a short time upon your affirmation, then say – *And thus, I stand.* Feel the spiritual strength of your intentions.

If you read the above a few times, you will automatically put in the pauses to fully identify with each line, and the more powerful it will become. It is a major affirmation and so carries the power and the will – use your will when you identify with it. It will keep you steadfast and on track. You will stay at the centre of the circle, and everything will go on around you.

© Andrew Carter July 2023

Knowledge and Wisdom

I have mentioned that only you can expand your consciousness. No attunement can do it for you. I give you a statement: *"You are an initiate before you are initiated."* In short, you have to reach that level of the initiation process before the initiation is bestowed upon you. There is what is called *the Rod of Initiation*. The Christ presides over the first three initiations, then it is Sanat Kumara, the Lord of the World. The third initiation is the one that breaks you out of the prison, so to speak, although you would have already done so. These initiations are something that go on upon the inner planes. It is good to be informed of them, but do not dwell too long upon their meaning, as it will be confusing. Just remember, you are working upon more than one initiation at the same time, for example – if you are working towards the third, you will also be working on the fourth and scooping up the left-overs from the second hence why I say it is confusing. It is not for the abstract mind, which can incorporate many things into its thinking.

Let us consider what stops you upon the path of initiations. Firstly, do you realise its importance? Do you realise what it means to you, and what you will achieve? So, before I talk about what stops you, can you now ponder upon what difference it will make to you. Very difficult, as you are pondering something that hasn't been attained, as such. But to an extent, you have attained it. It is there below your threshold of consciousness, waiting to surface, to rise from out of the depths. Ponder this from the aspect of the soul and use the '*as if*' you have already achieved the expansion of consciousness that goes with initiation. What will it give you, and what will you do with it? Leading question, but a disciple has to ask these things. I will remind you to retain a sense of humour – don't take yourself so seriously. It may surprise you to hear we don't take you seriously. You may also be surprised you hear you are further along the path than you think you are.

You may say you haven't meditated much in a week, and have been busy doing other things, or there has been a crisis you are having to sort out. That may be so, but mostly this is related to physical activity. What about your mind? Can you initiate the spiritual activity of the mind? Can you be at the centre of the circle? You can bring your soul into your physical activity. You can spend a week without sitting down for meditation, and yet during the day you are meditating, you are aligned just the same as when you sit down for meditation. You will come to recognise this.

© Andrew Carter July 2023

Knowledge and Wisdom

Recognition is a key word at this time - to recognise your part within the Divine Plan. You may have heard this before, and now you are hearing it again. Consider as you look out at environment and the happenings of the times – what does your awareness tell you? Once you have considered that, it would be worth considering your part in the Divine Plan in the light of your awareness. Through that, you will definitely realise you have a part within the Divine Plan and are impressed by the ashramic consciousness.

Now you have realised more fully than before, I want to go back to what is stopping you upon the path of initiation. This is not a special path for the chosen few. It is a path the whole of humanity is urged to seek, and you are that bit farther along than most. Because of that, you are fully aware of what has been stopping you, and a large percentage of that is yourself. Now you have worked with this presentation, you will have been brought to the surface and you will realise that the result of what stops you is a depression of the etheric body, creating lack of motivation. That is understandable considering the energies you must encounter and what plays upon your etheric body. Also, problems can cause an overactivity of the lower chakras. The depression of the etheric body keeps the chakras within the lower consciousness of those bodies, so they can be overactive on those levels and underactive upon the higher sub-planes which the chakra represents. The spiritual activity of the head centres then will not enter in to the brain consciousness, and you will put off what you need to do today until tomorrow, then another tomorrow. You do not, for long, put off washing your clothes, loading the dishwasher, otherwise things upon the physical plane becomes a mess. Relate that as an analogy to your spiritual activity. Pause now to give that some consideration. It is always worth manifesting your thoughts upon these matters.

To lift the etheric body out of its depression is to bring in light and become motivated. Bring that light into your aura and chakras – the light of the soul, the light of Divine Intelligence, the light of Divine Love, and the light of Divine Will. Feel that light – it will lift the vibrations of the lower centres, stimulate the head centres, open the heart, which will renew your spiritual activity, lift your consciousness away from the non-essentials, retaining the essentials.

© Andrew Carter July 2023

Mostly, it is your relationship with yourself and others that stops you from that spiritual activity. Part of you does not want to pursue your purpose, so I bring the word *recognise* into your thinking. How many times have you decided to pursue an activity and it comes to nothing? Your soul waits, the Master waits for your recognition. You can analyse yourself as much as you like, but until you recognise the true you, you will run around in circles and block out the truth, because your awareness will come from that part of you that is stopping your spiritual activity. It will stop you thinking about it, it will keep you thinking about all those things that are non-essential, it will have you running all over the place in the name of helping others, and doing many things of a materialistic nature. The lights I have mentioned will cleanse your energetic bodies - just like washing your clothes and then hanging them out to dry in the warmth of the sun. You can meditate with the warmth of the sun etherically and physically, with the heart of the sun, from the soul, and from the central spiritual sun from the Monad. Be inventive with your meditations and ponderings. Let go of the mind, be receptive to doing nothing by resonating with the space.

You will then recognise aspects of yourself that are holding you back. You have some idea of what the goal could be, so cut the ties from that aspect of yourself as it takes your power away.

I seek the light

I seek the way

Lifting my mind up to the heavens

To seek my true spiritual self

In the words of the Master M of the First Ray – *just get on with it.* They have a sense of humour. Have you a sense of humour and the will to just get on with it? Recognise what is holding you back, then drop it and get on with it. Do not be serious about yourself or others. It is the others you also have to cut the ties from in the light of the soul. It is not done from the personality – that would be a disaster, especially if you exercised the will of the personality from the solar plexus. You would be wielding force from the will and power of the personality, which would be control, to control your environment, and that is not the way. I am sure you can recognise this aspect of the personality.

How do you recognise emotional ties from others? Just study yourself in relationship to others and also, have you a tie to them? This doesn't mean pulling away from someone – it means you can happily interact without feeling any responsibility or need to oblige them. You have to weigh this up regarding the effects upon your spiritual activity. Sometimes we are brought to a standstill for whatever reason, so consider what you would do if that were to happen. When you are on the path, there are no coincidences. You will come to recognise this, and you may marvel at the way they suddenly appear.

You cannot hold yourself back forever – well, you could, but what is holding you back if you are on the path will get worse until you recognise what it is. You may have to become humble and drop to your knees to release what you are holding on to. Opportunities will come for you to recognise many things. There will be coincidences that will prove to you that you are going in the right direction. Fully relate to these coincidences and do not brush them aside with a lack of understanding, as you have all the understanding. Believe this to be so. If you put your love and will towards something and begin to bring it into activity, then you will be supported in your efforts. Be flexible and be prepared to slightly change direction – insight will come regarding this. The planet Mercury relates to the intuition and also the Plane of Buddhi – it is the magical messages that intuitively records what needs to be done, but be prepared to be flexible as the intuition may bring a spark of insight when you least expect it.

As I have mentioned, we are in a phase of transformation, a period of change, hence is seen a rising up that wishes to counter that change by bringing in glamour and illusion. Never more so is this apparent. This represents a very short period of time as the consciousnesses of many are gaining much awareness, and will not be lead like sheep. Any fixed ideologies are being challenged. Step aside, my brother, and go about your business in the light of the soul. Engage not in the petty quarrels that have no substance on earth. Take care not to lose your identifications with the planet Jupiter – love and wisdom – which also comes into the Plane of Buddhi.

© Andrew Carter July 2023

Knowledge and Wisdom

The seven sacred planets form a seven-pointed star in the heavens, with the sun at its centre, the receiver of the seven streams through which these planets relay. You are familiar with them. View the seven-pointed star via the One Life, just as you view your seven chakras as being part of your One Life, and, of course, the two sevens are interconnected. So, realise this when you visualise the seven-pointed star in the heavens.

The Solar One Life is also part of a greater One Life and is a centre within that One Life, so there are seven solar systems that form a cosmic seven-pointed star. This One Life is said to be the one about which nought can be said, at least not for now. We are breaking the barriers of time and space, realising a higher consciousness does exist all the way to the Absolute. Life is a parable of vibrational consciousness. Seek the sound of its mantric verse. Align with the seven in the heavens and turn your attention to the streams of consciousness. Listen for the sounds of consciousness, and through those sounds, create a mantric verse. Your first attempt may prove futile, or not, but keep trying. Make your attempts over seven days. The mantric verse may come in small parts over those days. If one day you receive nothing, it is not a waste of time as you are being overshadowed by the seven. This approach alone will challenge you, and you may question yourself in many ways. If you do, remember that I have relayed to you this might happen. What if you only get one letter? Would you deem that insufficient? Your whole personality will gain from just going with it, and, of course, the challenge from the personality is to actually attempt this for seven days. It may forget in the busyness of your life, and you may also wonder what to do with the mantric verse if you get it. And wonder how you know it is a mantric verse. Such are the doubts and questions of the personality.

Does any of this resonate with you? You are all capable of receiving a mantric verse, and in doing so, you have materialised the verse from the heavens into the physical world. You have brought its vibration into manifestation, so the vibration of the mantric verse would have descended through the mental and emotional planes into the etheric physical. Now, you can visualise this happening, and sound the mantric verse upon each plane, which will have an effect upon that plane and the glamour and illusion that exists, then the counterpart of those upon the etheric physical plane is called Maya. the pull of the materialistic focus. You can go back to the seven in the

© Andrew Carter July 2023

heavens to create a mantric verse for a specific purpose, such as healing. This you can do for yourself, but remember – anything for the self is also for others to benefit from, so always have this in mind.

Many methods of healing will be revealed over the coming years as they already have over the last decades. All those reading this presentation are healers in some way or another, and many more healers will emerge. You will have the knowledge to promote healing. Consider your place within with the Divine Plan regarding healing. Do not hold back - there are people in need. Also, bring in the knowledge and the wisdom to reassure people in what you are doing. Silently go about the task of healing – you will become magnetic and draw people to you. Just affirm to yourself the sacrifice you are prepared to give towards healing. Your sacrifice is your time and energy, your commitment to help others.

There are many ways to heal, even just with the spoken word. One sentence can relieve a person of all their worries. You will be inspired by a soul-to-soul resonance for that one sentence by an alignment with the higher consciousness, just the same as you received the mantric verse. Give encouragement, and be prepared that some may not listen to your words. They will hear them, but give no response. Again, this will challenge your personality as you would wish to have a response, but sometimes it can fall on deaf ears. This has nothing to do with any inability you may have. Some may say *they are not ready to hear those words*. If you want to use that statement, you can, until you realise what is happening in a different way, so ponder upon why this should be from a detached spiritual perspective, and go deeper into what the words *they are not ready to hear those words* implies.

I have brought this to your attention as the statement implies a superiority over the person it is being said about, that it has no depth of understanding and is a way of dismissing the person, but if you have risen above the personality, or better still the soul has integrated to a larger extent with the personality, then you are influenced by the Triad and possibly not make any statement at all. This is spiritual acceptance of a non-separatist nature, and the reason for this is your sense of knowing. There is no need to work it out, because you know what that person is struggling with regarding their spiritual journey in relationship to their life and environment.

© Andrew Carter July 2023

Knowledge and Wisdom

The sense of knowing is a state of silence, a silent knowing which you have all experiences, and will experience more of. Ponder this sense of knowing. It is an identification for you, for those times when you just know, but have no need to speak about. Some will ask you to speak about many things, but your knowing will only give you what you need to say at that given time, and that will be of an up-lifting nature and could be a very basic impact, and yet you know – a silent knowing. In relationship to this, it is worth considering the various circles of the Ashram from the periphery to the inner circle. They do depict a level of spiritual attainment, and as you move closer to the inner circle, you will be moving in to silence because you have attained the silence and your personality drops away and has no presence within this silence.

> I can relate to you from this silence, your sense of knowing. Can you take your mind, which is also soul, to the Ashram and visualise the Ashram and imagine you are entering it?
>
> Can you move towards the centre, slowly through the circles, each one becoming more silent?
>
> You can attempt the inner circle where you will find the Master. As you do this, relate the experience of silence to knowing.
>
> Your reward of knowing will come as you start to experience the different levels of silence.

Use your approach for seven days and you will find that you will be automatically drawn into the inner circle. You know where the Ashrams are, so there is no formal meditation for this approach. Just like the rest of this presentation, you are asked to create your own. In fact, it will create itself. You don't have to work anything out, and don't do any thinking because you become The Thinker, which means you bring something into your brain consciousness that you want to know, or that you have found of interest. You become The Thinker then there is a switch between your brain thinking and your brain being impressed, hence the Thinker doesn't think at all – not from the brain consciousness. It would be worth re-reading what has been said

© Andrew Carter July 2023

about the Thinker, then apply that to your sense of knowing. You may get some interesting results the more you attempt this. It can be used for many things, particularly if you are becoming a healer and Teacher. The identification with being a healer covers many aspects of life through your kind words. You are a healer because those words will heal someone's thoughts and feelings, and people just want acknowledgement for what they are going through. Just a simple '*I understand*' is enough. You can place your hands upon their shoulders and that contact will bring succour to their need. Sometimes there are no apparent answers. An answer can resolve an issue. If an answer is from a need to resolve an issue that is causing a mental and emotional problem, then it may not be the answer as it would have been thought about whilst in the emotional and mental state of wanting to resolve the issue because it is causing a problem.

The comfort of the personality seeks to resolve issues. Have you even been in a position where there is apparently no answer? How did that affect you? Also, was it your issue, or an issue someone else had that was affecting you because of your close relationship? Ponder upon how many issues since you have been on this journey have actually been yours, other than the spiritual acceptance of yourself. You may have recently had a rough time, but is that rough time of your making? Also, ponder upon cause and effect. Think too about before you started this journey and the difference in yourself between the two states – before and now you are upon this journey.

Issues always have an energetic interplay between everybody and everything that is involved. Bear in mind that there can be spiritual issues, but initially we are talking about everyday issues. Couple this with a spiritual issue, then that will stop you moving forward. It will stop you manifesting and you all know this. I seek to remind you of what you know. Sometimes your place within an issue is one of silence, allowing the energetic interplay of its component parts to play out, which will create an opening for an answer to descend. It is very difficult, as some issues are of an emotional nature and quite upsetting. I just ask you to try and stay at the centre point of your circle. Physical life can be unforgiving in the way things happen. Always think about the Ashram in those times of distress. There are other disciples who will come to your aid – let not the light grow dim. There is much to do – realise what you do has a more far-reaching effect than you can imagine.

You have attained self-consciousness, and as you observe, you must see there are many who have not this self-consciousness which you have worked so hard to attain. You will probably argue that it was worth putting in the work and making the necessary sacrifices. At this point, I would like you to realise your achievements. You have foregone the comforts of the personality and made the effort, whilst they may stay comfortable within their circumstances and they wish it to be so, but also many are wanting to attain something more although they know not what that something more is. They just sense and feel that the comfort of the personality is not enough. Something is calling them from beyond time, creating an unease of their situation. It could be called a personality unease. Yes, but also a spiritual unease. Something is starting to influence them, other than the world they live in; they are starting to realise there is more to life than what they are living. This is the influence of the soul, and the soul brings light into the mind. It creates a pathway to the heart and goes still further down through the lower centres creating a conflict with the comfort of the personality, and, of course, part of the personality is the ego, which likes to be in control. I will mention here that the ego, many years ago in esoteric writings, was known as the soul. It is not so now. I say this just in case you get confused if you read older esoteric books.

Before you started this journey, did you feel an unease and a definite pull towards other things of a spiritual nature? Before you incarnated, this was destined to be, but as humanity has free will, you might not have taken the opportunity. Now the next step is there for you to take - this is your destiny – and this destiny is taking you over to the next lifetime. Nothing is lost, and there will be much more to gain because you have overcome many challenges and so they will not be presented again. You are heading towards a continuity of consciousness instead of a lifetime consciousness. You have sacrificed the comfort of the personality for the light of the soul, and through doing this, your mental and emotional bodies would have been brought into alignment with, firstly, the ray governing the personality, and then the ray of the soul. As your lower bodies and chakras function through the personality with a duality, they are affected by the duality of the ray that governs them. Everything upon the physical plane becomes a duality. If you have knowledge of the rays, you would work out what that duality of effects would be. I suggest a study of the duality.

The manifestation of the ray of the soul within your consciousness has no duality, and so it will transform your lower bodies to become a positive aspect of the ray that governs them. In fact, they will become subordinate to the ray of the soul. Have you noticed how you have transformed over the years? You could study the rays to find the ray of your soul, but that would be difficult as you will find attributes of all the rays to confuse you. Bear in mind that through the soul comes the spiritual triad, and that alignment to the triad (in the first instance, the higher mental), is the next part of the building of the Antahkarana. First, consider what happens when the soul and the ray of the soul goes into the lower chakras and bodies related to them.

There may be a similarity of rays to the soul, or quite different. Can you imagine Ray One, mental body, which is the power ray, receiving the ray of the soul, which is Ray Two, Love and Wisdom? The result would be both rays working together, but there would occur a transformation of the mental body. Love and wisdom would be the major influence, not without some sort of conflict within the consciousness of the personality who, for a period of time, would be confused as all the thoughts the mental body has accumulated from the past would be challenged, because love and wisdom from the soul would come to the heart, then down into the solar plexus which is related to the mental body, then to the sacral related to the emotional body, and say that is governed by Ray Four, harmony through conflict, which on a personality level is Ragas and Tamas, high activity, low activity. The affect after a period of uncertain feelings would produce a dramatic change, bringing harmony and love into the emotional feeling nature, also wisdom, and would enhance creativity.

This is just one example of the effects of the soul coming down into the lower bodies. Can you imagine the effects upon the ray of the physical body and the activity of the physical etheric body? Think for yourself what ray that could be, and ponder upon the effects of the ray of the soul – love and wisdom.

So, you have reached the stage whereby the soul has brought a positive influence upon the lower bodies, and remember, this relates to consciousness and the psychology of the chakras. There is a two-way flow between mind and soul. Now what comes into the soul is the consciousness of the higher mental. It does not directly come into your mind and brain consciousness, but via the soul as you have now created a two-way flow. This does not mean that because you achieved this you will not have problems. It does mean you are better equipped at solving them as you will have become more inspired by the soul. Part of that soul consciousness will come from the higher mental. What does the higher mental mean to you? How do you see it? You could, at this point, meditate upon the higher mental to gain some more insight. You are aware it does not relate to a super-intellect. It does relate to intelligence, therefore, it is abstract thinking, creative thinking. Were there two aspects when you meditated upon the higher mental?

Some aspects of the higher mental are coming to you via the soul, and you will be losing some aspects of time that can so rigidly govern you. That does not mean *not to be on time*, just a sense of timelessness, yet you live in the moment, although you can look back and forward via the journey of the soul. You may be losing your sense of age and you will suddenly find a zest for life because of the creative ideas that will start to come into your mind. Now, because you have created a two-way flow with the soul, you will be functioning upon the higher sub-plane of the lower mental related to that sub-plane via discrimination, which you will be developing. Have you noticed you have become more aware and able to make better choices and decisions?

There is no direct contact from the lower mental to the higher mental. Now, because you have created the two-way flow with the soul and certain aspect of the higher mental are coming into your consciousness into the higher sub-plane of the mental, then you will start to create a thread of light across the gap that exists between the lower and higher mental. The higher sub-plane of the lower mental will connect to the lowest sub-plane of the higher mental. This is the next stage of the building of the Antahkarana, or Rainbow Bridge. This continues, and the bridge starts to strengthen, and is built with the seven colours of the rainbow and rays, and a two-way flow starts to be created.

I asked you to meditate upon the higher mental. In that instance, it was via a contact with the soul. Now, there will come a point when you will not need to do that because

Knowledge and Wisdom

you are becoming, in the words of the Master R, *a conscious soul incarnate*, so you go directly from the lower mental to the higher mental. You will become more impressive to the consciousness of the higher mental and what will happen is that consciousness will travel down through the chakras. To fully understand that, realise there is a counterpart of all your chakras within the crown chakra, the heart being at the centre. Have you noticed the changes that are occurring because of this?

Now I ask you to meditate directly from mind to higher mental via stillness and space. You can imagine a thread of light between the two, and then create more threads of light. You are aligning your mind with divine intelligence. A record of your experience would be useful. You will find it rewarding to do this more than once, so that you accomplish the next stage. This is simply using stillness and space which, by now, will automatically occur – this is open-eyed. Use your power of thought, which is no thought at all, but magnetic thought that brings about impression from the higher mental. What do you need to know from the higher mental? You can see how useful this is for your creativity. Place something into Divine Intelligence – you don't have to imagine placing it there, just think about something you wish to expand. Have you a project? Of course, from this level there is a relativity with the Divine Plan, and as you know, you have a place within the Divine Plan.

If you have given this your attention, you will become more receptive to spiritual impression – these days it is called *channelling*, which is slightly different to mediumship, which gives readings from those departed, mainly upon the astral plane, for, in some cases, contact with someone they loved, and also to give a message into the way forward. Sometimes a medium contacts a higher plane, so a message has no identification with a person, as such. Channelling also makes an identification mainly, for example, with the Angels - some sort of galactic identification - and is normally a message for the many. A term used is *light workers* or *light body activation,* and many other things, I have been brief with this. There are numerous variations of both mediumship and channelling.

Now, spiritual impression tends not to identify with anybody, as such, and does not proclaim, so it comes from the spiritual triad, the Divine Plan, and the Ashram. Yes, people have identified with Masters, but you won't identify with a Master, a Master

© Andrew Carter July 2023

will identify with you. That is the difference, and worth pondering upon. Also, you will be impressed by the Ashram itself, meaning more senior members of the Ashram, and some of these may be in incarnation. It is a fine line between knowing where you stand and where you think you stand. There are many who think they are further along the path than they are, due to those extra-planetary identifications. You may also think you are not as far along the path as you actually are. Do you believe you are in contact with the Ashram, or even a Master? Ponder upon these two identifications I have made.

The Ashram and Masters are upon the Buddhic plane, but the personnel of the Ashram are also upon the physical plane, nevertheless you cannot see the Ashram and Masters. If you did, it would be an astral counterpart that has been created, not the real thing, for want of any better words. There are also Ashrams upon the higher mental plane. In fact, they were all upon that plane until they moved up. This is evolution - as a vacancy appears, so someone is moved into that role. Before I continue with this theme, how do you know you are part of an Ashram that you cannot see? It's simple. If you can sense and feel the silence, then you are part of an Ashram, because that silence is what you experience within the Ashram.

Now, if you think about it, there are four sub-planes of the lower mental body. You have your consciousness upon the highest of these four; the next is the sub-plane of the soul which you have contact with because you are functioning upon the highest sub-plane of the lower mental bodies. The next two sub-planes are above the soul in the higher mental where some Ashrams reside, so they are not far away. In fact, they are very close to your consciousness and, of course, these Ashrams overlap into the Buddhic plane.

> Sit in silence, and within that silence and the eternal space, elevate your mind towards the Ashrams. You will find the vibrational frequency. Can you feel this vibration and stillness, and yet have an alert mind?
>
> Remember, you have built the threads of light from the lower mental to the higher mental. How have your achieved this? Well, you have let go, or I

should say – dropped many things below your level of consciousness that are now incidental to you, and do not warrant your time and energy. In fact, they will seem so *other* to what you have become. You have become free of so many things, and so your consciousness will naturally be receptive to ever-increasing frequencies. This creates an expansion. If you know the silence, then you will know many things. It's just a method of getting used to receiving them. You have to train to do that, but the more you seek to understand, that understanding will come to you. You will gain knowledge and cultivate wisdom. The problem you have is the lack of self-confidence in this respect. You receive impression and wonder how that happened. Well, I have explained this, so the words '*I don't know where that came from*' will not apply any more. You know where it comes from, so keep tuning into the silence and identifications, and then you will be a natural flow of impressions and you will think nothing of it - just part of what you do. You have to break through the barriers and put some time into doing this without expecting results – they will come!

You have bridged the gap into the higher mental, which is part of the spiritual triad. They form a triangle.

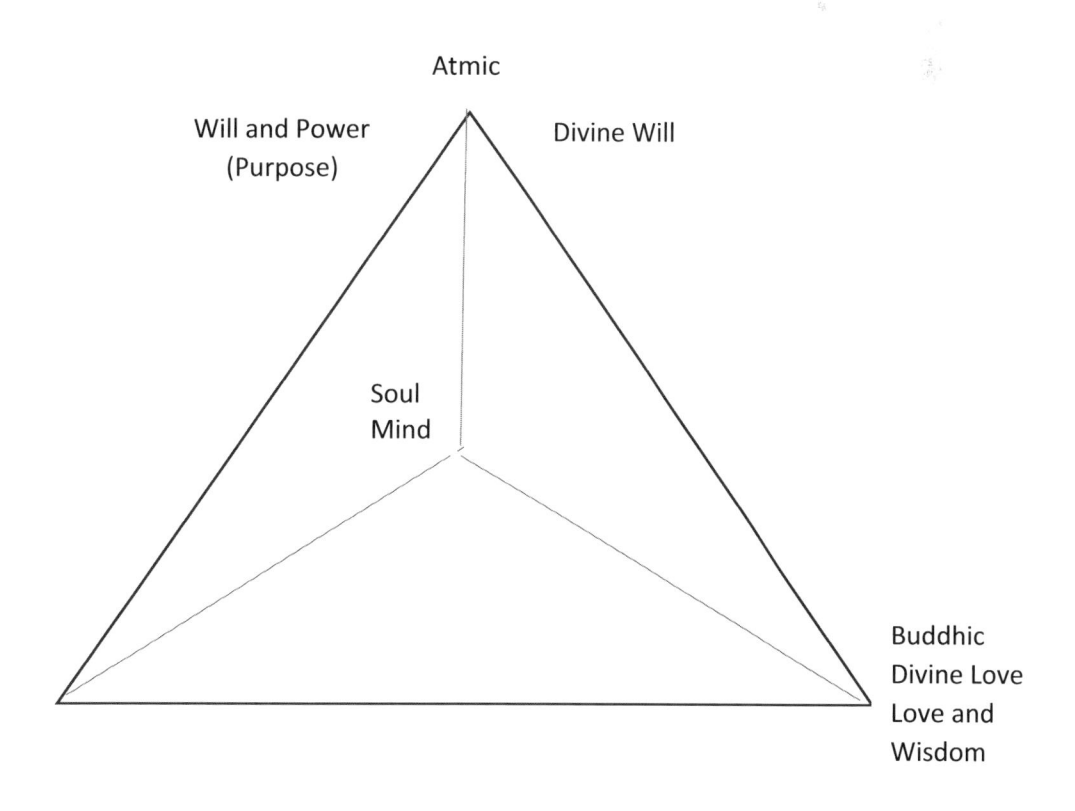

```
                        Atmic
           Will and Power    Divine Will
             (Purpose)

                    Soul
                    Mind


Higher Mental                              Buddhic
Divine Intelligence                        Divine Love
Active Intelligence                        Love and
                                           Wisdom
```

July 2023

At the centre I have placed the soul and mind, the mind relating to the brain consciousness functioning upon the highest sub-plane of the lower mental body, but it is in unison with the soul. The soul lotus has nine petals, three each representing each of the divine aspects which unfold, so the soul comes into the mind. The mind magnetically attracts the soul body in the gap, then becomes directly influenced also by Divine Plan, Love and Wisdom, and Divine Will, Will and Power, and Purpose. Your head centres will receive these energies. Head centres are crown, brow and alta major, which form a triangle. Many of you know this as it has been part of my teaching, but it is well to refresh your minds on this subject. Bearing in mind what has been said, normally this information is kept on an intellectual inspirations level. This time, make these alignments:

> Two-way flow, mind to soul, the highest sub-plane to the lower mental bodies, create that energy flow, then down through the centres.
>
> Pause and prepare to bridge the gap. Your attention goes to the higher mental via the triangle of head centres, which have become magnetic. Stay with the higher mental, then bring the energies down through the chakras.
>
> Pause then approach the Buddhic plane. You have bridged the gap. Pause upon the Buddhic plane, then bring the energies down through the chakras.
>
> Pause, then approach the atmic plane. Stay with that centre of will and power and purpose, then bring the energies down through your chakras.
>
> Your time with this exercise will be governed by your focus and stillness of receptivity.

I kept that very simple. Study the triangle first to become familiar with the energies so that you can identify them in the exercise. I have not written this as a meditation, but it is for you to turn it into a meditation. Once you have achieved that, a regular use would be profitable. An important factor is that your head centre becomes open and receptive. This will allow for a free-flow of energies from the spiritual triad into the lower centres. You all know they are found upon the etheric, and more outward into the bodies, and become a bit like a cone. It is according to your level of consciousness how far they have penetrated the bodies and are functioning on that level. Not everyone's chakras function upon the highest sub-plane of the mental body. As an example, when you form a relationship with the soul, they will penetrate the causal body of the soul. Remember, a subtle body (for example, the causal body) surrounds you. What happens is the chakras increase in vibration and that vibration becomes the same frequency as, for example, the causal body of the soul, The chakra has added another frequency to them, which then drops down into the lower sub-plane of that chakra. This applies to all the chakras, but the vibrational rate of the new frequency is also slightly different for each chakra and will relate to the consciousness of the chakra and its function.

This may all sound very abstract and it requires a higher mental mind to get to grips with it, but if you throw away the logical three-dimensional mind, it will make more sense. A diagram is not possible unless certain rates of frequency are placed upon it. You can know what all this means without logically working it out. You could possibly re-read what I have said and bypass the logical mind to see if you get a sense of knowing, and through that sense of knowing, use your imagination to perceive energy interaction. Remember, everything overlaps and crosses over. Imagine the different vibrations of the chakras, the frequencies, and the sounds. Bring the spiritual energy of the space into these interactions. Do you wish then to focus upon your higher head centres, then pursue further interaction. They can be of a planetary nature or a solar nature. Be inspired, not forgetting your connection to the earth.

This connection to the earth is so important. You are connected geometrically and energetically to the earth's energies, which are also geometric in nature. Through your study of sacred geometry, you have become familiar with the earth grid, an icosidodecahedron – two platonic solids intertwined then turned to form the earth grid, the lay lines. The crystals are geometric in nature - seven crystal systems. Your aura is geometric in nature - it is two interlocking tetrahedrons, another platonic solid.

© Andrew Carter July 2023

Remember, all these are formed for a sphere, which displays the number nine, not to mention the golden mean – 1 to 1.619. The 1.618 reduced equals the number seven.

Ponder upon the number seven. Imagine the light geometries of the earth. This can follow on from what you have previously just imagined, remember that in your feet are secondary chakras.

You are magnetically held to the earth via your etheric body. The earth can give you strength as you stand, sit, or walk upon it, so ponder upon the yin and the yang – earth and sky. You can reach up to the sky, the spiritual world, whilst being fully earth conscious, and these energies, the yang, will come down into your consciousness to the earth. You will be connecting the earth to the planetary spiritual. The earth aura is connected to all the planets of the solar system via the etheric space, the so-called *veil*. There are also etheric planets within this space.

Are you using your imagination at this point? You are connected energetically to the earth and to the spiritual plane of this planet, and also to the planets via their association with your centre system. You are much greater than you know yourself to be, so that greater self, your overshadowing spiritual soul, will give you a vision, and in line with that vision, a goal.

Let me give you the keynote of the Sagittarian full moon – *'I see the goal and reach the goal, and then I see another'*. This, you are starting to become aware of. You may have many ideas, and this is a positive sign of your contact with the higher mental. In fact, you may have too many ideas as your idea expands massively, so it becomes unattainable. You can work with more than one idea, but use time wisely. You think you don't have the time and wish to manifest something almost immediately. The downfall is also to work out its material needs. Instead of working out what you should be doing, why not ask what the Masters and the Divine Plan want you to do? That may be in line with what you are inspired to do.

> At this point, take your focus up to the Masters and the Divine Plan. Hold your focus there.

© Andrew Carter July 2023

Knowledge and Wisdom

> Whilst holding that focus, bring into play another focus upon humanity and the need of humanity. Hold that dual focus.
>
> Now put yourself at the centre point between the two. Is what you are inspired to do in line with that dual focus.
>
> I leave you to take it from there, and to gain insight into your work.

That is worth repeating, because all too often you play down what you wish to present. For example, many will not understand this – it is beyond them and they find it too difficult, so I need to keep it more simple for their understanding. Was it that way for you? Did you find what you didn't understand of great interest and wish to know more? Do not hold back your knowledge and wisdom. Be prepared to speak about these things. A common saying is that people are not ready. You cannot be the judge of that. They may appear to be not ready if viewed from their personality interactions and communications, but they may be ready on the level of their soul. Also, ask yourself – am I ready? If not, why not? Always bring the light of the Ashram into what you are inspired to manifest. The biggest thing you perceive are obstacles to what you are trying to manifest. You judge people for their lack of commitment. You worry nobody will take up what you are trying to do, even though you are upbeat about it. That still lies within you.

The thing you have to actively engage in, what you are manifesting - you have to give it energy. Be excited about it and tell people. Let go of the drab conformity of telling people. Create this with your excitement. You also worry about what people will think about you, as they have not your knowledge and wisdom, and they may find it strange. All these things you think about. You wish to boost your self-confidence, not lose it, so you have expectations, yet those expectations are met with a fear of failure, which may also have been a problem with you in the past. Society functions upon success and failure. This also governs children. You have been brought up in that duality. Society is trying to correct that, but not in a spiritual way.

© Andrew Carter July 2023

Knowledge and Wisdom

Competition does not have to be based upon success and failure. People may have been disappointed with you in the past, and you may have been disappointed in yourself and say, *'I could have done better'*. Who, or what, is saying that *'I could have done better'*? It also depends on how you say it. This is the great misconception of speech – same words, but carrying a different tone of energy. Ponder upon some words and how they are expressed to gain some understanding. Play with this – do not skip over it. Also, do not rush through this presentation, seeking to finish it to go on to the next thing, or because you feel you should have finished it by now, but have not. You may read the pages as rapidly as you can, so you can say to yourself *'I have finished this book'*. Something to think about. Also, the Master R, in his teachings, suggests to read the content without trying to understand it, with the mind completely open, then go back to read it to gain understanding. The first time of reading it will be dropping into the sub-conscious because there was no intellectual barrier preventing it from doing so. It then will precipitate up into the mind, your understanding will be enhanced, and you will embody the concepts.

It is so important to give positive sound to the words you speak and also, through that, the positive feelings connected with the words. Do you feel the words you speak? Attempt to feel the mantras and invocations you may be using, and also, the will behind the words as they are expressed. Find out what expressions the words contain and sound the words with the energy of their meaning. Avoid speaking the words in a horizontal manner, especially spiritual words, the words of a meditation, of insight, of poetry, of meaning for another person. Once more, practice sounding words. They carry a vibration – you are all aware of that. Embody the words. Ponder upon the word *embody* and its meaning.

Realise also, your name is your identity and you wish not to lose that identity, so say *I AM* and your name. Bring in the will, but not in an aggressive manner - just enough to establish yourself within yourself. Your name makes you who you are. You were given that name at birth, and not by chance. If you think about it, when your name is spoken, people know who you are – they identify with your identity. You wish them to make a positive identification, and not be spoken about in a negative way. If your light shines bright, then when people identify with your name, they will receive this

© Andrew Carter July 2023

light, and probably feel uplifted. So, how do you feel about your name, the one you were given at birth? The soul gave you your name. The name was given to you by your parents with maybe influence from other people, but where was the real influence coming from? Give a thought to the energies present on the day you were born, and also the time. This relates to your astrology – we have discussed astrology. When you are born, these energies impregnated your etheric body, giving you a predisposition to certain characteristics. The energies present at your birth relate to the constellations and the planets. Consider also, what was present were the energies of the rays, which concern consciousness, which also impregnated your etheric body. These energies impregnate the spiritual sub-planes of the etheric body and predispose your ray life. Through your own personal development, you come to access those ray energies. Your duality then starts to fall away and life is seen through different eyes, through the eyes of consciousness, intelligence, love and will, hence you become the Observer and your ray life develops automatically, taking your consciousness into the solar system.

Memory is also stored in the etheric body which, at an early age, is fluid and needs to retain its fluidity until a certain age of development. The need during the first seven years of life is not to develop the child's mental memory faculty. If it is developed, then a fixity of the etheric body occurs and the soul is taken away from the child because the soul is part of that fluidity and is a major influence upon the child. The soul influence for us is through the head centres; for a child it is through the etheric body. If it is maintained with the child, then it continues into the next stage of development. The soul then continues its journey upon the earth plane. Rebellious children can be soul-inspired - something to ponder upon in relationship to yourself and your perception of life through the eyes of a child and their circumstances.

Always bring the light of the soul and, also for you, the light of the spiritual triad into your etheric body. You will loosen all those stuck strands of early memory which, for you, can hold you down into the lower worlds of consciousness. They can be a block, so it is worth considering if there is something from your past conditioning that holds you back, even though your understanding goes beyond that conditioning.

© Andrew Carter July 2023

Knowledge and Wisdom

> Bring the light of the triad, one aspect at a time, into the etheric body – first intelligence, then love, then will, down into your etheric body, into its line of light that intertwine and also interpregnates the physical body.
>
> The line of light also creates vortices - the chakras. Use your creative imagination in the process of transmutation, then bring the triad into the mind. Much will come from doing this exercise, and you will also overcome the effects of the planets upon you.

If you study the rays, it would be useful to know that a ray governs each of your lower bodies. It is written these bodies that the rays govern, enter into duality, but if those bodies were governed by the soul, then they become a positive influence upon the lower bodies. Through that, knowledge becomes wisdom. Knowledge is a building block for an expansion into the many facets of what that knowledge represents. Take the knowledge, and want to know, then more knowledge links to existing knowledge and expands into wisdom, and penetrates into the unknown, which is beyond knowledge. Can you expand your knowledge into the unknown without knowing what it is? This requires trust, a trust that the unknown will enlighten your mind to become known. Always the higher worlds seek to impress the lower worlds, to uplift its consciousness, to effect change towards the evolution of a more perfected humanity.

Why not try to expand your mind into the unknown beyond time, beyond the physical. Part of you exists beyond the physical, but what are you seeking? The answer is *nothing*, because if you are seeking *something*, you will not enter the unknown. Your mental body, with its *something* will not allow you to go beyond it. Some seek nothing, but expect from the unknown something – have no identification as to what it will be. What if you get nothing from the unknown, are you going to give up and have doubts as to your ability to receive something? This is the human condition, and if this exercise into the unknown was attempted in a group, can you imagine the outcome? This is not something to attempt in a group unless the group is an existing spiritual group that has created its group centre of light because then the ego would not be present, nor the doubt.

© Andrew Carter July 2023

I have mentioned before about the time equation. Have you understood that your impression may be received later in the day or at a later date, and also that impressions may not relate to the unknown as it did not occur whilst going into the unknown? You may have been impressed by the unknown and then it may have taken an amount of time for it to precipitate into the conscious mind, so if you were asked in a group what you received from the unknown, could you have said *nothing* and still retain your self-confidence regarding your identification with the spiritual? All these questions are worth asking to give you realisations and enhance your approach to the unknown. I could give you many identifications for what lies within the unknown, and I have already given many, but for this exercise, no identification is more rewarding.

You may have just experienced silence within the unknown and a total resonance with the space you are surrounded by, so you would not have anything to say about the unknown other than the silence. The secret to the unknown is this silence. Until you have experienced it, you cannot come to know it. It is possible you have experienced it in meditation, but I say to you that when you came out of meditation and had nothing to say, then you have experienced the silence of the unknown. Questions may come at you - *'What did you get? What was your experience? Would you like to share?* There will be those only too willing to share, but you will not want to say anything, and that will indicate the success of your meditation.

As a healer, you work with this silence. You have an awareness of the space, the awareness being that all is ever present within the space. Let us consider what that is. There are seven planes within the planetary life. There is the familiar physical, etheric, emotional, atmic, and mental. Within the higher levels of the mental are the causal (soul) and the higher mental (intelligence). Further still the Buddhic plane (love). We are within the spiritual and atmic (will). There is also the Monadic (love and will), and the logoic. All these planes have sub-planes and different frequencies. All these vibrational planes exist within the space.

© Andrew Carter July 2023

> Sit for a moment looking into the space that lies between the objects, with a relaxed glaze. Bring into your awareness that all is ever-present within the space. Particularly realise that the spiritual vibrations are within the space.
>
> Now identify with your aura, with the spiritual vibrations of the space. You can experiment with closing your eyes.

With that exercise, you would have felt the vibrations and the stillness. What happens is the lower vibrations of the space drop away and you are left with the higher vibrations of the space, the spiritual energies. Just a realisation of this as you gaze into the space will produce the stillness. Look into the space and see the silence. You will then feel the silence and you can do this at any time of the day, and with it you will have a totally clear mind. That is then a good time to ponder. Consider what you would like to ponder upon. Many insights and inspirations occur during the stage of pondering. Have you a project, or something you wish to expand your consciousness into? Repeat the previous exercise and then enter into a period of pondering. At some point all this will happen naturally and be automatic. The energies of the space will be conditioning your aura, opening up your head centres for a greater receptivity. Your vibrations will higher and you will be within stillness.

I have mentioned the word *conditioning* concerning the aura, which relates to how the spiritual energies react upon the aura and condition it, increasing the vibrations of the lower bodies and releasing negativity. This also has an effect upon the chakras, and in turn, the endocrine glands, and the blood stream - just by looking into the space. We are conditioned by many things during life and that makes us what we are. Some of these energies that have conditioned us over the years get in the way, so to speak, of the evolutionary spiritual development your soul is seeking to impress upon you. We are entering a new era. It is unavoidable as different energies will be affecting our consciousness, and remember, these different energies are part of the evolution of humanity to enter into the Fourth Kingdom – the Kingdom of Souls, a fourth dimensional reality. We have been conditioned by the Sixth Ray and all the values and rules that ray has given us. Remember also its duality.

© Andrew Carter July 2023

Knowledge and Wisdom

You have already risen above some of that conditioning, and you see others who have not. You see this ray still impinging upon the consciousness of humanity through the mass thought-forms that have been created by humanity. You are reaching out for freedom from this conditioning and becoming more conscious of the rays that are gaining in their potency. You only have to ponder for a while on what this past conditioning represents. You may see it more in others than yourself, and this is one of the reasons for you not wanting to engage with certain things and people – because they are conditioned by the past character traits that have been handed down to them, or have affected them, producing a certain defence or rebellion as a result. The old way is not the new way. Things all continue from the old way if they are in line with the change in consciousness and the Divine Plan.

One aspect that is of the old way is control. The more there is control, the more laws there are to exercise that control. With this, I am talking about humanity, but also you can think of that statement as an individual who seeks to control. What law does that person implement to keep control of his life and, indeed, with that of others? They will not be written laws like the laws of the land, but that person will wield the arm of the law over others and themselves. Control takes away free will. Humanity has, from a spiritual perspective, free will and from that level, it cannot be interfered with, although certain forces seek to do that. So, part of your conditioning is control. How do you control yourself? Through past conditioning. What do you stop yourself doing? what so-called values have you that are part of this control? Remember, we are moving into something new, and a person five hundred years from now will not understand, to any great degree, a person of today. Also bear in mind that conditioning which you probably take for granted.

Relate that conditioning to something you might be sensitive to, not necessarily of an emotional nature, although it could be, but of a mental nature. Your memory contains your conditioning and so does your etheric body and chakras, but you also have your mind that is impressed by the soul. I have presented before the concept of a transference between mind and soul. A simple case of using your space exercise, then focusing into the mind centres of the head, then the soul above the head creates a symbolic representation. Place your mind into the soul then, and the soul into the mind, thus creating a loop of energy. Very quick to do if you have entered

© Andrew Carter July 2023

the stillness that the space exercise creates. You can then ponder upon the conditioning, or it may present itself to you as you have just identified with the concept by reading the exercise prior to the transference of energy. I suggest just throw away your past conditioning, because your past conditioning will reflect in your expression within the world you live in.

We have talked about control, so the control you exercise over yourself through past conditioning you will exercise over others, and that may well be in very subtle ways. Control is not just a power-play of force – it can be subtle. Lawrence McCafferty mentions in his book *The Heart of the Mystery, The Tiger and the Monkey.* The approach of the tiger concerning control is quite obvious, but not so the monkey. The monkey apes and will be a good friend, do things for you, until such time that it has you under its control, then the demands will probably be of an emotional nature. Be aware of the monkey!

Try to imagine you are just you, with no past conditioning. Do not try to throw away what is you (hence my suggestion of using the transference exercise), or you may throw away aspects of yourself that are deemed inspirational. You, as a personality, cannot discriminate these, but as a soul you can, and so you will become more joyful, uninhibited, freer, and more liberated from the responsibility of yourself that you have controlled through past conditioning. You will become less serious. Take what has been said into your consciousness – this is what you seek to achieve. Then, through a transference, take what you wish to achieve and bring the light down into your etheric body and chakras, and release yourself from control.

Control can come from Saturn, the equivalent on the Tree of Life is the Sephirah Geburah, which relates to discipline. Disciple of a spiritual kind is very different to the discipline of a physical nature. The word has a relationship to control. Saturn itself is the planet of Karma, cause and effect. Our journey started on Saturn, and the energies passing through Saturn are Ray Three (active intelligence). The earth itself is governed by Ray Three (active intelligence). This was the result of the evolution of humanity upon the moon chain, whereby humanity there was seeking to embody active intelligence therefore, it was passed over to the earth. We are seeking to

© Andrew Carter July 2023

Knowledge and Wisdom

embody love and wisdom, and part of that is to relinquish control, as control will hold you to the planet of karma - Saturn - and the influence of the moon.

A third factor here is the planet Mars. I have mentioned that governs, for everyday humanity, the solar plexus, whereas love and wisdom govern the heart centre. Have you seen the importance of the heart centre for uplifting your consciousness out of the solar plexus into the heart? The solar plexus is nevertheless your power house of energy within the physical world, and that needs not to be depleted. You require that energy to motivate you into spiritual action. This is what is required – spiritual action – not the passive state when you can spend hours in meditative silence, seeking your own state of bliss for your own benefit. Spiritual action relates to the Ray One energy of will and power and the crown chakra – from love and wisdom to will and power. With those two, your identification is the Monad, but let me add to that, from love and wisdom, will and power,

Ponder about what has been said about spiritual action. Take what I have said into meditation and pondering with a focus upon the Monad. Seek to know the Monad. Also consider that cosmic love and wisdom is the source for the Seven Rays. They have come from cosmic love and wisdom and been separated into seven streams of consciousness, and yet they are not separate, as such, because they come from one seven. Consider then yourself as coming from one source, therefore you are not a separate being – you have an individual identity within non-separation. Do you feel separated from your spiritual essence?

Many of you are realising your connectivity through chance and circumstance, because you are relaxing control, you are seeing it for what it is and wish to have no part in it. You will stand outside from it. You will remain quiet and cease to engage, and yet in standing back, you retain your spiritual power because you do not want to control. Your consciousness goes beyond those who seek to control. You use the truth and see no reason to explain yourself – and why should you? You have taken responsibility for yourself. Others do not see the need to be responsible for their actions, particularly their self-expression. They do not take responsibility for what they say, and give it little thought.

© Andrew Carter July 2023

You are responsible because you are conditioned by the soul and spiritual triad, and your eyes are open and not blinkered by an environmental conditioning. You may be realising quite a difference between the people on the path and those who are not, but also realise there are many of goodwill who are seemingly not on the path as they know not what you know. They are on the path, but have no realisation if it, but they wield the energy of goodwill and are non-separatist and, in a way, are further down the path that those who know themselves to be, but who are still enthralled by the glamour and illusion. Their personality creates success upon the spiritual path and they employ materialistic means to achieve it. Even though they are seemingly successful, they have achieved success by being clever. Many will see through the mask they portray.

I give you the word *humble*. In this respect, humble is not a lack of power, it is a recognition of something far greater, so release all the power of the ego and seek nothing in return. Yet, there will be a return if you do not seek it. It is the law of giving and, of course, there is receiving. If you want nothing for yourself, then you are humble to that which spiritually impresses you and surrounds you. You can engage with the environment with no agenda. Stop reading and attempt to do the following exercise.

> So, ponder upon the word *humble* in the light of your spiritual experiences. Have they touched your heart?
>
> Does your heart open to the spiritual compassion, and do you feel humble as you stand face to face with your soul?
>
> This is a Second Ray experience and yet behind this is the ray of will and power. You have to expand your mind to come to know this, so by being humble, you can expand your mind.
>
> I leave you to do this.

© Andrew Carter July 2023

Knowledge and Wisdom

I have mentioned rays and you know they travel, so you can reach out into the solar system. As you are approaching the Monad, this is a potential you can achieve. Remember the seven, the three, and the one. I remind you once more that the heart is the centre of the seven – three below and three above. Then there is the soul, which has three below and three above. Then also there is the Monad which has three below and three above. I have not mentioned these – it is for you to realise the potential expansion of the number seven, so ponder what has been said. Even higher threes go beyond the cosmic physical plane.

All that is spiritual and all that is material regarding the earth and its plane of consciousness are part of the cosmic physical plane, so consider then the next is the cosmic astral plane, which overlaps upon the Buddhic plane of Divine Love. Always there is an overlapping, with no separation between the planes. There is no separation of all the aspects of your being, physical or spiritual – it's just that many do not engage the spiritual and, in a way, they have no method to do so. This you have to realise. You are here to teach them how to find the spiritual in real terms. The spiritual has to come down into the physical and manifest upon the earth. Enlightenment is not rising out of the physical altogether. Enlightenment is achieved upon the earth whilst in a physical body. Many seek to discard their physical body for their light body, but do they understand what the light body is? There may be many names given to the light body, and also beautiful pictures to stimulate your ideas of what it is.

Well, you have three light bodies, not one, all while is physical manifestation, so let us imagine this. Surrounding your physical body is the etheric body, but it also goes inside the physical body, so there is an etheric counterpart of everything that exists within the physical body. Then realise the etheric counterpart of the nervous system, and just above this is what is known as the *health aura*. This is a protective layer of the etheric body and combats heat and cold. It also protects from negative energies, so if you can, imagine all that has been said and realise also the impregnating lines of light of the etheric body.

Connected to the health aura and just above it is what is known as the *etheric light body,* so you are surrounded by the etheric light body, which is golden in colour - just

© Andrew Carter July 2023

imagine that. You can imagine its penetrating and weaving energies of light also within the physical body, you can imagine the centre point of light at the centre of every chakra. Now, cast above the head to find the nucleus of the soul whilst keeping your imagination upon the etheric body of light. The nucleus of the soul is within the causal body, which surrounds you. This is the soul body of light and is white light. Can you imagine this? You can also imagine this white light moving towards the etheric body of light through the lower mental and emotional bodies where it meets with the etheric body of light, and then white meets the gold.

This has given you an understanding of two of the light bodies and you have brought the energy of the soul body of light to meet with the energy of the etheric body of light. You have brought the light of the soul into the physical. Not only that, you have brought the soul light through the lower mental body and the emotional body, and that would have a great effect upon your thoughts and feelings. So, this is worth repeating as an exercise to stimulate your spiritual self and dispatch negative energies, and become more aware of the soul. This also created the conditions for a greater contact with the higher mental aspects of intelligence.

There is a third body of light. I have mentioned the intelligence that exists beyond the soul, the higher mental. The second is the Buddhic plane of Divine Love and Wisdom, which I have also mentioned. The cosmic astral plane overlaps the Buddhic plane, which is part of the cosmic physical plane. Consider that the cosmic astral plane on the level of the Buddhic plane is etheric. Ponder upon that in relationship to the physical etheric. It is also said that the Masters live in their Buddhic light bodies – yet another body to try to consider. Just for your information, there as Masters of Wisdom and Masters of Compassion, just as upon the atmic plane some work with the will and power, and others with the will and purpose. Then we have the Monadic plane, the home of the Monads, and there you will find your third body of light – the monadic body of light.

The previous meditation exercise focussed upon the etheric body of light and the soul body of light. With the information just given, can you now incorporate into the realisation exercise your monadic body of light? The Monad may present itself to you as a symbol. Remember, this body of light surrounds you on the periphery of your

© Andrew Carter July 2023

aura. Awareness of the soul and the plane above leading to the Monad is via a higher vibrational consciousness. Ponder upon the meaning of higher vibrational consciousness – a consciousness that goes beyond the veils of time. You are physically within time, yet your consciousness can go beyond time, and when you integrate the soul, you go beyond time. Have you a sense of timelessness and yet time goes by and you remain as the soul – timeless? This is the silence within the space. Try to reach that state at this moment in time. If you are experiencing silence (and that can be achieved anywhere), then you have gone beyond time. You have entered into a high vibrational consciousness and you can reach out in consciousness towards the Monad and activate your monadic light body. It is at this point when you can be impressed from beyond time, and also, you are at a place of healing.

Everything upon a physical level – the body, the mind, the emotions – have come to rest, so to speak, and in that state of rest, they can heal. This will happen even if you are not aware that it can happen, but if you are aware, then your consciousness itself will be allied to the healing energies. You can utilise this in many ways. Just use your creative imagination, which is a way of directing energies to what you seek to achieve. It is important that you stay with the consciousness of the soul, not the personality, with any directional intent, otherwise you will drop back into time and a lower mental functioning.

> Lift yourself into a higher vibrational consciousness – stay within the silence. You slowly go beyond time. All your physical bodies become totally inactive. This is the place for healing and intuitive insight.
>
> Which do you require at this moment?
>
> Within the silence you become magnetic, attracting the higher vibrational energies. If you are searching for insight, stay within the silence, then bring your proposition into your mind and wait in anticipation.

© Andrew Carter July 2023

Remember, beyond time, it may take time for you to register an expansion of your proposition. If it is healing, then it would be useful to imagine a sphere of healing energy above your head.

You can visualise energy from this sphere coming down to your head centres and from there, use your imagination to direct that energy.

I leave you to take the direction you require to achieve the silence.

I wish to present to you *The Seeker, The Thinker,* and *The Discoverer.* You have to seek to discover, so, for example, on the physical plane you have to go off-track to become the Seeker, and then, through that seeking of new experiences, you discover many things, I am referring to going out into nature, to the villages, to the ancient buildings. There are many wonderful things to discover, but you have to learn the familiar routes to find them. This can also be related to the mind – to go beyond the familiar and become the Creative Thinker to create stories, poetry, and all manner of things. You have to want to seek. Yes, you can seek knowledge, and that is useful, because what you discover will anchor on to the knowledge you possess and it will also expand the knowledge. You can expand your knowledge by thinking, not only researching. It is so easy these days to just Google what you wish to know, but you have to discriminate the real from the unreal. It is best to have a knowledge of esoteric science as a foundation.

So, to enter into a higher vibrational consciousness is to become the Seeker. Never be satisfied with what you have attained; never sit back thinking *'I know enough now;* never circumscribe yourself within a particular method of learning. Always seek beyond the horizons, yet retain your earthly connection – your sense of humour. A higher vibrational consciousness has a sense of humour and does not move away from earthly life to seek its one salvation and ascension. When you seek, you seek for the many all too often. It is for the self – that is all right if what is discovered for the self is also related to the many. This then becomes a selfless act because in self-seeking, there is a lot that others would benefit from. Do not be afraid to speak up about your discoveries. A higher vibrational consciousness always projects outward

© Andrew Carter July 2023

upon the horizontal plane. This is via your vertical approach, and then there you sit at the centre of the circle at the point where the two lines cross the vertical and the horizontal.

Once you attain a degree of resonance with the higher mental, then the seeking becomes natural, or an automatic reaction to a soul inspired consciousness, then you will become the Thinker. What do you think about? Well, the higher mental will naturally inspire you, and that could be at any time of the day. If you try to work too much out intellectually, then you will drop down to the lower, and lose the higher mental inspiration. You will be entering into a lower mental activity.

Now you have all achieved a degree of soul consciousness, and I have presented the Seeker, at this moment become the Seeker. Realise you can discover something, so you slowly become quiet and still, and enter into the silence of the space as the Seeker. You can affirm '*I am the Seeker*'. You wait in anticipation, with no preconception, for an impression. Once you have an impression, then become the Thinker upon the impression. Your aim is to discover more from the impression. Keep relaxed with an empty mind, so to speak, but your mind is the mind of the soul. Realise your mind is of the soul. It is also the mind of the spiritual triad, which lies above the soul. So, seek also into three higher realms of consciousness, then become the Thinker once more. Always seek to discover.

Isaac Newton was asked how he discovered the Law of Gravity, and the answer was: –'*All I did was think about it.*' It is worth remembering that he never researched it, he just thought about it. At times, turn your attention away from the material world and become the Thinker. Realise you have the ability to discover, and one of the biggest things you will discover is your true self – that pure, unadulterated self. This doesn't relate to your physical form. To understand that, become the thinker. '*Unadulterated*' means that spiritual self unaffected by the progression of life through the physical world of distortion, hypothetical values and the world-wide glamour and illusion. Can you imagine your progress in life if the Kingdom of Soul was present upon the earth? Most people are not ready for that event. There is much still to learn, but if that was so, would you not be where you are today? With the abundance of the soul, you have entered into a totally different consciousness – a consciousness that

© Andrew Carter July 2023

is perceptive. Use your perception wisely and do not turn it in upon yourself, or outwardly as negativity towards others with criticism and judgement. You will get to a place where it appears as if you don't care, as others will not get the reaction they require from you, their needs you will not be met because your perception sees through their glamour and illusion, and you will not engage with it.

In real terms, you care more, but you don't criticise or judge, so you wouldn't engage in other criticism and judgement, and they will think or even say *'You do not care.'*. What you have done is discriminate the situation. You have discriminated society and your true-self will be engaging. You cannot be something you are not. In the past, you have tried to please, and that pleasing of people will be seen as you caring. Yes, there will be an aspect of that, but also there will have been a part of you that wanted to be liked and accepted. Now that is disappearing, and may be completely gone. You see the world through cause and effect, and yet your complicated mental activity has given way to the soul and higher mind. There is space within your brain consciousness, there is time to think about other things.

Your power lies in your silence, not your action, and yet spiritual activity requires action and directed focus upon that activity. Power is not control. If you cannot control anything, then you can enter into a spiritual activity.

The last paragraph is worth pondering upon from within the silence and peace of the soul. Can you do that at this moment in time before reading on? Record your insight.

One insight you may have gained relates to control. You can allow the flow from the spiritual to guide your action and direction, and also influence your thinking. Control and concrete thought. More and more we are being guided to rise above and be open to new concepts, to be spontaneous in every given moment, to be inspired and open to change direction according to what is presented.

It is time to move on from the past, its conditioning, and its out-dated methods. Do you want to stay fixated upon a certain philosophy, or a spiritual method of development, or certain healing practices? Discover your own wisdom from the wisdom itself. You are part of a spiritual centre. It is there to inspire you to bring its light down into the consciousness of humanity. You have created a pathway into that spiritual centre of light, and yet it is difficult to realise it within everyday life. Take a few minutes just to make an identification with that spiritual centre of light. Create your ashramic approach. You will be entering your relationship with it. You can try that now, before you forget what you have just read. It is an approach to the Buddhic plane. How will you make your approach? It is via the compassion within your heart and the love of your soul. Remember, once you have identified, there will always occur a two-way flow of energy.

I have not complicated that approach. You just have to attain silence, then imagine the spiritual centre of light. Yes, I could name many spiritual centres of light and guide you through many approaches, but it has to be simple so that you can make that identification at any time of day, thus creating a resonance with your soul and mind. You can, upon retiring, make that approach if you can create a repetition, then, because of that repetition, it will become natural to you. We are influenced by repetition, and a lot of the time it is unconsciously. Give some thought to how repetition has influenced you so that you automatically play it back.

Look at speech. Consider your parental influences, your environmental influences. A repetition will act upon your sub-conscious and then you will repeat it back. So, how much of what you say is not actually you, but a repetition from somewhere else? There is positive repetition, but there is also the negative. You see, all this repetition imprints your etheric body. It weaves into it through memory, therefore, it influences the chakras, which are centres of consciousness, a reflection of your consciousness and also your influence. What we are working towards are spiritual influences, the rejection of the negative, an expansion of consciousness, a dissolution of negative repetitive influences.

You have probably become aware of such influences as you have become self-conscious. Your self-consciousness has discriminated those particular traits that are not you, that have become part of your sub-conscious, and you have brought them up into the conscious mind and dealt with them. I give you an analogy of listening to your favourite song. Look how it then repeats itself in your mind and you have trouble stopping that from happening. It is the same for what is said to you. If it is repeated, then you have a memory of it. It may not repeat in your conscious mind,

© Andrew Carter July 2023

but it will in your sub-conscious mind, and if what is said to you is of a negative nature, then that will affect you in many ways. There are two aspects there if the negative is aimed at you, or it's a negative repetition concerning others or environment and that concerns certain words and sentences that suddenly you find you are repeating, and this will be automatic, especially if there is little self-awareness.

What is aimed at you can have a devastating effect upon your *'I' identity* - the person you really are - and those negative statements will affect your entire state of being. We have to be very careful what we say to a young child. Rudolf Steiner quotes that there should be no forced methods of committing knowledge to memory until the age of seven, but we should tell the child as much as possible because they are still in a fluid state of receptivity.

I will briefly mention the development of the chakras is consciousness –

0 – 7 years   is the base and relates to security. This is a time when a child is very receptive

7-14 years   relates to the emotional aspects and creativity, the sacral

14-21 years   is the mental body. This time period is where a child learns very quickly, if they have not been forced to commit too much to memory in the previous years. It relates to the solar plexus, which is the centre of power, hence the child wishes to be himself. There could be conflict

21-28 years   is the heart chakra, unconditional love, love and relationship, a more caring attitude towards others. The development ends with the crown at the age of **49 years**, then it goes back to the base –

49-56 years   and expands itself. This is where past problems can repeat themselves, so, for example, if there was a major problem between **7–14 years**, its effects can repeat at the age **56-63** years.

© Andrew Carter July 2023

If you ponder upon all this, you will see a relationship to what has been presented concerning repetition of a negative nature that has rooted itself within your memory. Let us not forget the positive here, and its effects in later years.

As you know, the chakras connect you to the solar system and the planets, and the energies coming through the planets, and obviously the planets themselves, but that aspect of influence you are starting to negate. It's those influences of the planets that makes you receptive to negative repetition as your centre of consciousness will become receptive to it. This is the difference between the ordinary wheel of astrology and the reverse wheel, the reverse wheel negating the negative aspects of your astrology and the planetary influences that created it.

There is a danger that you block off your emotions concerning this negative repetition. This is part of the human defence mechanism that can break down and the emotions become overwhelming. Always remember, the higher governs the lower, and so it is through illumination and self-consciousness that we come to learn so much about ourselves. In this learning, it has to be from the positive so that you can negate those things and enter into a higher consciousness. When I say *negate,* it doesn't mean you will never think about your past in a so-called negative way. It will happen, but you will have an understanding of what is happening, therefore, you will not be overly affected, and move on from it. You have to remember you are human, after all. It's a matter of whether negative repetition and emotions affect your work and your spiritual progress.

Remember also, never be satisfied with what you have attained. You can feel good about it, but always realise there is more to reach out for. Your meditation work is an important part of this, along with whatever your development has come into expression. Many see the expression as being very hard to implement and get disappointed if things do not take off the way they had envisioned. Maybe consider your approach could be of a materialistic nature, as you have self-doubt and not the will to push it forward, and you may stumble at the first hurdle. Instead of being disappointed, gain from the situation, become more fluid, do not push it out to other people for your lack of response.

© Andrew Carter July 2023

Knowledge and Wisdom

Many reading this work will be attempting to get things off the ground. Blend your will with your love and then employ intelligence. Be prepared to be inspired. What are you attempting to do as you read these words? Think about it. Also, what should you be attempting to do? The Tibetan wrote about the lethargy of disciples and their lack of will. An easy option may confront you, but consider what you have learnt and the needs of humanity. You can do this now, at this moment in time.

> Consider what you have learnt. Do this in a meditative state of pondering. It would be useful to record your reflections.
>
> Now cast up to the sphere of spiritual light, the ashramic consciousness, then the need of humanity in relationship to what you have learnt, and your reflections upon it. You have formed a triangle.
>
> Record whatever insight you get - you may have to wait until your mind becomes a nothing. You may be surprised - do not dismiss anything. It may not be what you *want* to do and what you *want* to express, but it may be what you *need*.
>
> Consider that as you focus upon the ashramic consciousness upon the Buddhic plane.
>
> Then bring your love and will into action upon your insight, then the intelligence, which will guide your way.

It is worth revisiting this meditative approach to build upon your first attempt. This is repetition of a spiritual nature, so consider what spiritual repetition you have in place, or are they sporadic according to what is going on in your life? There will always be a lot going on in your life, so you are required to prioritise, but you don't see yourself and your spiritual work as being important enough for you to partake in it fully to the extent you are capable of doing. Consider what gets in your way. Consider the essentials and the non-essentials. That may not be something you wish to do as it is very down to earth, but the earthly things are so important for your spiritual growth.

© Andrew Carter July 2023

You cannot have your head in the clouds seeking help from the Angels and wishing to ascend from this earthly life. The object is to bring the spiritual down to the earth, not to escape to the spiritual and leave the earth to just get on with it.

The Ashrams on the Buddhic plane are in the process of incarnating, and that is through you. They wish you to be upon the earth as long as possible for this to happen. This incarnation will be through the groups of disciples upon the earth – you have to aid with this process. Also, a great Avatar is approaching and can only go as far as the mental plane at this moment in time, bringing in totally new energies – the energies of synthesis. So, become receptive to those energies.

> Ponder for a while upon what has been said within the silence of the space. Become a magnetic centre for the incarnation of the ashrams and then sense the approach of the Avatar.
>
> Attune then to the energies of synthesis. In doing so you are bringing these energies into the physical world. What do these energies mean to you?
>
> Remember, these energies are new; they have only been sensed. Reach out towards them.
>
> Give them a meaning and a purpose. Bring them into your mind. Let them work through your aura. Seek out their mysteries.

These energies require a totally different way of thinking, and bring a radical change from the old ways of thinking and being. Understanding will come through awareness – you just have to sense them and they will touch your consciousness, and things will change. Remember, you are a *disciple.* This is not a word I like to use in this modern age, but I cannot think of another that depicts your relationship with the Masters and Ashrams. You may think you haven't got a relationship because you feel you could be doing more, and you are not advanced enough to be called that. This is your problem and lack of self-recognition – it is not a problem the Masters have.

© Andrew Carter July 2023

> Take a moment within the silence of the space. Negate all though, become a nothing and request the ashram to give you a colour. Request the Ashram to give you a word, and then request a number.
>
> There may be more than one colour, word or number. Record them and then ponder upon them.
>
> If you received nothing, start with requesting the light of the soul to illuminate your mind and imagine this. Then make your requests.
>
> Remember, each colour, word and number have three aspects relating to will, love and intelligence. You can add that to your pondering.

Quite a lot to ask of you, but this is the way of expanding consciousness. The more you do these things, the more the answers will come - in mysterious ways. At times they will defy logic and the intellectual mind.

Can you go beyond logic, the linear mind that only defines duality, for example a yes and a no? That is the logical mind – a yes or a no to any given question or subject of discussion. *Yes, I agree with that,* and *No, I don't agree with that.* This is the 'I' identity of the solar plexus. An opinion is based upon this, and normally the yes and no is a spontaneous reaction to a given situation. Here we have to take into consideration the psychology of the 'I' identity in relationship to the psychology of the chakras.

> Ponder upon what has been said and relate it to a situation you are familiar with, then pause and consider - is it a *yes* or a *no* situation? You may think it is.
>
> Then bring in the abstract mind, the higher intelligence just above the soul, so through the space you come to know soul.

Knowledge and Wisdom

> Then reach into the depths of space to find the higher intelligence. Then consider what else could it be rather than a *yes* or *no*.

You may have brought up a situation you were involved in, so you have a personal identification with it. This you have to put aside, otherwise you will only register the yes and the no, which you probably engaged with within that situation. I am asking you to go beyond yourself within the situation to seek an expansion of consciousness concerning the situation. To do this is to rise above pride, because pride will not consider anything other than the yes and the no is had initiated. It will see it as a backing down, a loss of face, and may even feel embarrassed if our expansion of consciousness reveals other than the yes and the no. Some people stick rigidly to what they have said, even in the face of being given proof that reveals otherwise. They cannot back down from what they have said as they would have lost face.

I am sure you have all come across what I have been speaking about – pride. You know the truth and they will not listen to you, and that leaves you frustrated, and maybe a little angry, especially if it concerns people that are close to you. The answer is to see it for what it is, so therefore you discriminate your activity concerning them. Also, ask yourself why you want them to acknowledge what you are saying. You will say *'because it is the truth of the situation'*. Understandable, but the more you expand your consciousness, the more all the lower ego tendencies will be revealed to you. And then what will you do? I hope you are understanding what I am saying, or may you, too, have an element of pride that requires rising above. You just have to step back. There is strength in being silent, and it takes a lot to be silent in certain situations because your personality will definitely want to respond. Your soul will be guiding you to be silent. You have to live the soul-life. You may have been hurt, but realise it is by someone who does not have your awareness and understanding. Why expect others to be on the same level of understanding that you have attained? You may say, *'I can't believe they have said/done that.'* Realise that is from *your* perspective, not theirs. It is wise not to put yourself in a position for all

© Andrew Carter July 2023

that to happen. This is the wisdom; this is why I am relating it to everyday life. Continuing your spiritual development requires you to know these things.

Through your spiritual development, you will naturally want to heal people. That may not be as a healer, as such, but through your connections and intentions. You would give insight to enable someone to rise above their problems, alleviate their pain and suffering. It will be natural for you to want to do this. All of you on this path of development are becoming more aware and are expanding consciousness, becoming healers, and as I have mentioned, there are many ways that come under the heading of healing. If through your interactions somebody feels a lot better mentally and emotionally through your ability of communication through compassion, then through the spoken word, you have healed that person. If you have advised somebody with your spiritual insight, then you have healed them from their personality problems.

I would like you to ponder now for a moment on all the times you have done that. The reason I am asking you to do this is so that you realise all the healing you have given over the years. All too often, you do not give yourself credit as you believe, to an extent, it is the ego. As mentioned earlier in this work, in some esoteric book from years ago, the soul was referred to as the ego, but today it means something very different. I do not want you to be confused if you come across this. Also, the soul in some works was referred to as the Solar Angel. The soul was not always there in the far distant past, as it is today.

So, your personality and what you may have read or experienced from others, will say that if you give yourself credit, then it is of the ego. This is false. Now, if you give yourself credit and then go out there saying how wonderful you are and proclaiming yourself as a spiritual Master, then that is different. If you met a Master upon the physical plane, and they do exist, you would not know that is what they are. On the Buddhic plane they have no personality bodies. On the physical plane, they have, but are perfected so there is no ego, no desire. They would not proclaim who they are, but just their presence would produce profound changes.

Ponder for a moment upon the glamour and illusion that those who set themselves up as a spiritual Master, and be able to discriminate between the real and the unreal,

© Andrew Carter July 2023

and whether, with them, there is humility and compassion, and is there the spiritual will that expresses truth? The true Masters do not seek to become popular. They might gain an extent of recognition, but it will matter not. Their work will be for the few. Do not worship idols and one philosophy. Those who worship one pathway will not step upon the higher pathway. Take what you can from the many pathways to then be lead to the higher pathway.

So, give yourself credit for all the good you have done. The Masters recognise this, so why don't you? Then you can accept, without pushing it away, the credit others will give you. Can you see the two-way flow here? Another thing that occurs is when you receive credit, you may say, *'It wasn't me. I was just guided from somewhere else.'* You must have come across this. That is another form of ego, and it negates any responsibility for those reading this book. You know where it comes from - it has come from you and through you. It comes from you because you have love and compassion in your heart for the person you are healing, therefore, through this magnetism, you attract the healing energies from beyond time. Yes, from the soul, but essentially from the Buddhic plane of Divine Love with the sense of touch, as it is related through the levels, becomes healing upon the Buddhic plane – and so you heal. As mentioned, this can be through speech, through the quality and love of the speech. Obviously, you can be amazed at what you say, but you know where it is coming from. If you give yourself credit and accept credit from others, then you will easily drop the statement, *'I don't know where it's coming from',* or *'where did that come from?'* You are a spiritual being living a physical plane life, and you recognise that, so do you now recognise that you know more than most people of the life of the soul, through your awareness and sensitivity?

A few words upon sensitivity. To some it is a problem, but in essence it is an asset. The problem lies if you consciously focus on the energies of the environment and other people. There is a lot of talk about negative energy, especially from technology, but also there are likes and dislikes concerning the energy of certain places and certain people. You don't have to overly feel these energies thereby affecting your energetic systems, because in doing that your emotional astral body will become too sensitive, and there is a great possibility of you being ungrounded. It is very difficult to put this across. Your protection from negative energies is your aura. Instead of activating your emotional body to sense energies, why not activate the soul and bring light into your aura instead? If there is something that is impacting you, bring the light of the soul down from above your head, down through the chakras. Then, from the crown, bring it over your etheric body, which is close to the physical, then flood the entire aura with light and stop sensing the environment, and consider why you would not do that. We know negative energies exist, but focusing upon them makes things worse. In fact, you may, through your sensing, attract more of the same kind of negative energy. This is worth considering and not forgetting. How does that happen? Well, I have spoken about identification. Your sensing becomes an identification, therefore, what you identify with is attracted towards you.

Sensitivity can be used in a very positive way if your emotional body, which relates to the love aspect, is connected with your Buddhic body Divine Love, which relates to the intuition, so you can sense something, Then, that which you sense is related to the Buddhic body and intuitively processed, thereby taking away the negative effects of the energy that is sensed. Remember, it is not your energy. Another question arises, why would you want that to interfere with your aura and emotional body? Because all bodies are intertwined, it all affects the etheric body. The etheric body underlies all your energies of the physical body, as mentioned before, so therefore your sensing could have a physical affect upon you. In your terms, you become an empath, but if you know why you have become an empath, then you can do something about it, unless of course you wish to stay that way. It is your choice. You may lose some of your communication to others – it will not any more become a talking point, but then your overcoming of that situation can become a talking point to others who suffer the same problem.

Always hold in your mind what you have achieved, others can also, and you will then have the ability of bringing that to their awareness. I'm not just talking about being an empath, but it is wise to discriminate who is ready and open to receive your knowledge and guidance. To some people, it all falls on deaf ears, but don't underestimate who is ready to receive your insight. You may be surprised if you pitch it towards their level of experience, and some of that you can call common sense – that which is quite obvious, but can be ignored. The pathway to the higher consciousness is not one of heightened visual experience. Yes, there will be mind

© Andrew Carter July 2023

Knowledge and Wisdom

experiences, and their meaning will be symbolic, although the logical mind will not interpret their meaning, but the logical mind will recognise the experience with a silent knowing.

Many will approach you with the logical mind, with questions: *What does that mean? What does that do?* and all sorts of things. You will recognise their need to understand, and so give insight based upon their need, and what their soul is urging them towards. The soul will be attempting to establish recognition within their consciousness. Sometimes, there will be a light-bulb moment and, of course, you must also be prepared that they will forget everything you have said to them, including the light-bulb moment, if they are not creating a change within their consciousness.

Life and environment is a very busy place and full of sound. You can be sucked in and forget all about our spiritual journey and it will take up all your time. Well, it could be perceived that way, but what is the reality of this lack of time? I will remind you that we use time to our advantage, not be governed by time with everything we do. I have mentioned this before. Create interludes instead of going from one thing to another, and your head becoming full of one thing, then another. If this is happening to some of you who are reading this book, ask yourself if you are happy with that. Then ask yourself that again after you have created an interlude. While your mind is fixed upon those things, then it will say *'but I have to do these things',* and not answer the question at all, and it will come up with many other reasons.

> Create an interlude, and that means use the silence and the stillness. Create your own stillness.
>
> Your eyes turn towards the soul, and through the eye of the soul, reach out towards the Buddhic plane and the Masters.
>
> Then ask yourself the question *'Am I happy with that?'* You can then ask what to do about it, how to get back on track.
>
> You are part of the Ashram and you need to move closer. Bring the light of the Ashram down to remove the fog of the personality.

© Andrew Carter July 2023

> Remove all responsibility, until there is just you, then bring the responsibility back in from the soul. It will have changed.

It comes down to not letting the logical intellectual mind rule your thinking, and being the governing factor of your consciousness. Once it is not, you will experience an expansion of multi-trains of thought, but not deva thought, a higher vibrational thought, interesting thought. You can play with that thought, leading you into creating a concept. Ponder upon creating a concept. Consider what a concept is. Consider an intellectual concept – facts, figures, documented proof, or whatever the concept is based upon. As you read that, did it have an element of suppression, a fixidity to your already expanded consciousness? Take yourself away from that type of concept and give some thought to a spiritual concept, and that can concern the physical worlds. Consider there can be a concept concerning the physical, the emotional and the mental aspects, but your influence for the concept will be spiritual. All you have to do is tune into the higher thought-currents. To do this, firstly – what is your interest, what do you feel passionate about, what is close to your heart? Then realise you can create a concept concerning this. You have the ability to expand and create a concept from within the silence.

This can be a challenge as you are getting towards the end of the presentation, or you might not be in a suitable position to do it. You don't have to be in meditation, for example when you meditate first thing in the morning. You just have to be silent wherever you are, and then think about an aspect of great interest to you. Then wait for a response from the silence. Remember, you are doing this for the many to give them the wisdom of your concept, and, of course, in this age there are many media outlets for your concept. Let the higher consciousness inspire you. Record your concept, which may only be a few words, then focus upon the words and you will find more words will come. Have no expectations.

Give it a go, before you read on.

The more you practice this, the more attuned with the higher consciousness you will become, and your flow of words will increase. You will be able to tell the difference between what is coming from the higher consciousness, and what is coming from the lower mental. Sometimes, a concept is expanding purely with the knowledge you possess. The more knowledge you possess, the more the higher consciousness can latch into it. I give you an example. Many of you know about the 30 years collaboration of the Tibetan with Alice Bailey. You may also know that the book was written by Alice Bailey through a telepathic link to the Tibetan. The Tibetan has stated that with some of the concepts he was relaying to Alice Bailey, there occurred a problem as there was no knowledge of the concept within her memory – there was nothing to latch on to. So, knowledge is useful as a platform to the wisdom, and in obtaining knowledge, for example reading a book, it is best to read within the silence. Do not try to understand everything the book is saying, because within the silence it will be going into your sub-conscious; the logical brain does not need to become a blank for this to happen.

Time is not a barrier, but you can make it so by allotting time to your endeavour, for example *'I have time at 3 o'clock tomorrow to create a concept.'* But the concept is already there. It doesn't know that you have given it a time slot. When you get to 3 o'clock tomorrow and prepare to receive a concept, it doesn't show up. You could then get disappointed. You have to learn the language of the higher consciousness and what intuitive thought is, and not separate time, unless you need to, which refers to your first thing in the morning meditation.

If I have already mentioned this, then I have been required to repeat it, because it is so important. You must have experienced a time when you have not meditated regularly and noticed the different between when you do. It is necessary to meditate before the day starts, then you will be in a position to handle the day as many things can occur during a day and, to an extent, can be quite unknowable, whereas at night, you would have been affected by the day. I do not wish to focus upon the negative as it could have been a positive day, but the danger of meditating at night is that you may fall asleep. You can use the night to observe your day from the soul, whilst taking on the attitude of the Observer.

Having just read that, did you meditate this morning or yesterday morning? You have to fully realise what it can do for you, but as always, time is involved. You may

© Andrew Carter July 2023

think a gradual process is getting you nowhere, but it is, so sometimes it is good to look back to see your progress, then to look forward to your future progress – your evolution into the One Life. The One Life constitutes all the planes related to the earth that lie within its atmosphere, within the space. The planes also lie within the space that is closest to the physical earth – what you move through on your journey through life. Can you move effortlessly through the space? This will be a reflection upon your journey. Life is but a journey - many lives, many journeys that make you what you are on this present journey. The planet itself is in evolution and so are we - the ability to evolve to become much more than what we are; the unknowable becomes the knowable.

Self-healing comes through understanding, and through your evolution and soul growth. The understanding creates calm within the emotional and mental bodies, and a release of tension in the physical body. If you cannot understand things, then there is a tension, a build-up of energy within those bodies. Essentially, self-healing concerns the past and the effects of the past. The present may be a problem, but the problem you have in the present will have been experienced in the past – not the same people and place, but your reaction to a present problem will have been experienced in a past problem. There will be an originating source that has carried your mental and emotional responses forward into the present. So, what do you heal? The past or the present? Neither. You heal the conditions present within the mind and emotions that have caused a reaction to the past and present, and when an understanding has been gained, the past and present are automatically healed and will not continue in the future, and so you evolve out of the personality into the soul. Thus, past problems will be seen as part of your evolution and growth towards your spiritual self.

To understand yourself, you have to understand others, and this is the most difficult thing for people to do. I have mentioned before the common statement, *'I don't understand why they have done this, and been like that.'* Consider this has been from *your* perspective, and this is part of the understanding – to take you away from yourself as being the centre of your own existence. Just think about the word *consciousness* and a level of consciousness. Where do you place your level of

© Andrew Carter July 2023

consciousness? Don't underestimate yourself at this point. Now, if you don't understand others, then you have reached a level of consciousness that is beyond theirs, but you expect them to have your level of consciousness. In essence, they have not, and that is not separatist, it is purely an observation. Were you not like them at some point in your evolution?

When you take yourself away from yourself, then you will understand others, but not in the light of purity. If you try to see things from that perspective, then there will be much confusion. It comes down, once more, to discrimination and realising we are in a transition period. It is very sad indeed to see the lack of self-consciousness as cause and effect always works out in duality. We live in duality. If your consciousness is above duality, then you can see this duality in the light of the soul, and not be deterred by it, because you understand it. Yes, that enacts self-healing upon an emotional and mental level; yes, that will affect the physical, so the statement is *'Understanding heals'*.. Motivation also heals – it brings in the energy of will and it generates you into action. It captures your interest and so it can take you away from your problems; it energises the chakras and endocrine glands, and indirectly brings healing to the physical body. All things are interconnected and certain aspects of psychology have an affect upon the physical body. Meditation heals and it brings you into a silence. All aspects of your mental and emotional nature relating to any problem drop away, because your triangle of head centres (crown, brow, alta major) are attuned to the spiritual.

I have presented three ways of self-healing – meditation, understanding, motivation. With these three methods, there is no need to focus upon the problem. Sometimes you will need help from someone else for your self-healing, as we cannot always do it ourselves.

In this time of transition with so much insecurity and lack of trust, what is also happening (and that is due to the incoming Seventh Ray) is that the crystals and minerals are coming out of the earth as they are governed by Ray Seven, (manifestation) and Ray One (will and power), consequently they are magnetic and radiatory, and they are being used for healing, meditation, and room spaces to name a few of their uses. The interest in crystals has rapidly grown and they have become

Knowledge and Wisdom

very popular, especially with the young, (this is 2023) so it is understandable why they are coming out of the earth to blend with humanity. They have a direct connection with the highest plane of Atma, which is governed by Ray One (will and power) and Ray Seven (ceremonial order and manifestation), so to say we should not take them out of the earth is not true for this particular time period. They are being brought out into the light, into the air and space as part of the evolution of humanity and the Planetary One Life. The universal geometries will bring harmony and peace, and connect you to the highest spiritual plane through their relationship to that plane. As involution proceeded, the spiritual was brought down to the formation of the physical, so it makes sense that the spiritual worked within the earth in the form of crystals and minerals are coming out of the earth as part of their evolution to connect to humanity.

Also, coming into manifestation is the Fourth Ray of harmony and peace - 2025. It is all part of the Divine Plan and even though they are innate and not able to move or speak, as such, they can create a communication with the spiritual worlds through their geometries. Also, their energy lies in their etheric body. They constitute a kingdom of nature and are not a random occurrence. All things can become known through a piece of quartz crystal, and quartz has the power to heal.

There are seven chakras and seven crystal systems. There are twelve systems of the physical body and there are twelve constellations. Let me add to the seven – there are also seven sacred planets. I have given you something to think about. You know each of the planets relate to a chakra. Can you also relate a crystal system, for example, the cubic system related to the base chakra? Attempt to find the others, but leave the logical behind as the trigonal system will work with triangles. The more you think, the more your consciousness will expand – thinking will become an everyday affair. Be aware – what you may consider a revelation, those of the lower mind will not understand, so do not judge them for this. There will be many who will, and now this is rapidly happening, people are seeking beyond the physical, looking for answers, looking beyond the mundane life.

The Divine Architect created the geometries of the crystals. You, too, can create; you can become magnetic for the creative energies of the universe. Your chakras are

© Andrew Carter July 2023

your connection to those creative energies as they are etheric in nature, and the etheric goes beyond the solar system in ever increasing rates of vibration. Become that which you have never been before, then your light will go before you. Yet, in the silence, we humbly bow down to the love that exists within the heart. Always keep that love within the heart.

> Enter into a silence. Feel the vibrations of the space. Take your mind into the solar system, which is held together through love. You also exist through love, so open your heart to this love, the love of the Creator.
>
> You wish to spread this love to others. Is there anybody in need of this love? Hold the love gently within your heart, then you can identify with who requires this love.
>
> Remember, love heals.

I hope you have engaged with that healing as it would also heal yourself. When you give healing, you also receive healing, and so that healing energy will be within your aura. It will be in the room space - magical things can then happen. This can happen more so now, as the Seventh Ray is gaining in power, and the Seventh Ray governs the physical plane, therefore, the physical body. It also has a relationship with the sacral chakra and the emotional body. Its colour is violet and it can transmute things rapidly. You can connect to the Seventh Ray.

> First, identify with the sun, as that is its travel to the planet Uranus, then to earth, to the Seventh Ray Ashram of the Master R upon the Buddhic plane of Divine Love.
>
> It has travelled from cosmic love, then a gradual stepping down of vibration to the earth's plane of Divine Love, then imagine it passing through the soul, then you can use the violet ray to cleanse the etheric body, spending no more

Knowledge and Wisdom

than a few minutes doing this, then be inspired. The violet ray is very powerful and rapid, so the whole thing will probably only take five minutes.

That exercise will completely cleanse the etheric body. The only other ray that acts with this speed is Ray One, will and power, the colour of red. Both these rays govern the Crystal and Mineral Kingdom, which is magnetic and radiatory, and it is through these radiations they can heal, but only, to the greater extent, combined with the energies of the healer. Their radiation becomes magnified when healing energy is channelled into your aura and the room. Bear in mind, it is already in the room, as all is every-present. Another factor is the soul of the client, who also brings into the healing its own energies of healing, which blend with the radiatory energy of the crystals. Can you imagine if you could see all those energetic interactions?

Do not underestimate the healing power of crystals and your own healing power. A lot of healing will be happening - you cannot see it, but you will sense it through the silence and the absence of time.

Can you move gracefully through time and space, or do you stumble around, attempting to keep up with life? Life and environment pose the challenges. They will create mental and emotional activity, and yes, you will feel uncomfortable with circumstance. What will you do? Employ the same method you have in the past, the same reactions, and want to bring about a solution? You could create repetition of past experiences and, to a degree, you will not be aware of it as you focus upon what is challenging you, and you will be searching for a solution. Realise you may jump into finding a resolution too soon, especially if the situation is causing mental and emotional activity. Your reactions will be based upon them.

Now, you wish to create a higher mental activity which will not cause any problems to your everyday mind and emotions. Realise also that you may be at a point of tension in soul life, and this is something different whereby all this activity you may be undergoing as part of tension, will result in a break in your life as a soul. Environmental situations are character-building for something greater. Stepping back is of great advantage, and allows time to bring about change. Observe this change in

© Andrew Carter July 2023

full consciousness. People are not aware of the energies and forces, particularly the beneficial energies that can come to your aid. The activity of the mental and emotional bodies affects the brain consciousness and things need to happen now. Think of cause and effect before you make a move. That is related to the planet Saturn whereby the Third Ray of Active Intelligence passes through its aura to earth. Consider employing Active Intelligence, not active intellect, to situations.

This Active Intelligence, as it lowers its vibrations, can, if you are not careful, bring more power into the solar plexus if your mental and emotional activity are reducing the activity of your head centres and the soul light. Ask yourself if you can step back. Can you wait for things to change the progress or descent of humanity into physical form started on Saturn, then to the Sun and Moon? Saturn is one of the seven sacred planets through which the seven rays pass. The Sun receives them from the seven triangles of constellation. The Earth is governed by Active Intelligence as that was what the Moon was trying to achieve. The Earth is therefore working towards love and wisdom, so the influence of Saturn greatly affects the results of our actions. When we consider the scale of Libra, then you can say Karma (cause and effect) brings about the balance for these actions. Time is involved but it is inevitable. It is said the Lipikas Lords are the Lords of Karma

The solar system, or the Solar One Life, has its own ways of bringing itself into balance, and the Solar One Life is approaching a major initiation and so that will be affecting all the planets which are part of its life and consciousness. The Planetary One Life. and particularly humanity, are being influenced therefore by the progress of the Solar One Life and, of course, humanity is also part of the initiation process. We are here to evolve, therefore, energies are coming to the planet to hasten our evolution, but they are bringing about a period of conflict. This always involves the conflict between the personality and the soul – the conflict within the self. It may appear to be an outer conflict, but it is how we mentally and emotionally react to the outer conflict, so therefore the two are one.

The First Ray emanating from Shamballa has made various direct impacts upon humanity. In the past, this energy was given first as an alignment – Shamballa, Hierarchy, Humanity - but the impacts now are Shamballa, Humanity, and this is part

© Andrew Carter July 2023

of the initiation and evolution of the Planetary One Life, not because humanity has arrived at its spiritual point to be able to receive these energies. This energy is will and purpose relating to your spiritual will and purpose, and to expand your consciousness to pursue that purpose with the spiritual will and power as your guidance. Of course, this will and power can be used for control as we live in a world of duality, and spiritual will and power can become materialistic will and power. Be aware you are wielding this energy with the right reasons - an open heart revels the truth.

Let me reiterate what is now going on regarding the ray energies. The Sixth Ray of idealism and devotion is rapidly fading out of manifestation. The Third Ray of active intelligence and the Fifth Ray or creative science are receding. The Seventh Ray of manifestation is replacing the Sixth Ray. The Fourth Ray of harmony through conflict manifests fully in the year 2025, and the First Ray is making random impacts upon the consciousness of humanity. Behind all this, the Second Ray of love and wisdom is always in manifestation.

If you meditate on what has been said with the knowledge you possess of the rays, then you will understand the state of tension that exists today. Realise also we have been influenced by the Sixth Ray for such a long time that we have developed patterns through that influence. All that is being presented here is to release you from those Sixth Ray patterns. It requires a totally different way of thinking. I have mentioned Saturn and the Third Ray of active intelligence in relationship to cause and effect. The solar plexus in many people is governed by Mars, hence the karmic consequences. When advancing, it becomes governed by Uranus, Sixth Ray idealism and devotion, but in the process, the transformation occurs via the Second Ray of love and wisdom, heart centre influencing the activity of the solar plexus. The case will be more so when the sacral blends with the Fourth Ray of harmony, and the devotion and idealism will rise up to a different spiritual level than was seen in the past, and the impacts of the First Ray will produce a heightened spiritual activity, a particular alignment. You can try this now.

© Andrew Carter July 2023

Heart centre (love and wisdom) to the soul centre above the head (knowledge love and will).

Back to the heart centre, down to the base chakra (harmony), then bring in the crown chakra (will).

You can now view this on a vertical alignment creating a two-way flow of energy.

Using that method will raise you out of the duality that exists on the lower planes – the lower mental, meaning the lowest four sub-planes of the mental plane – the emotional. That analogy to the mental plane can be understood regarding the emotional plane, then the etheric physical – all that is in duality, meaning there is a positive and a negative aspect to that which is positive. Above that fourth sub-plane on the mental plane is the causal plane soul. Here, duality falls away and everything becomes what it should be. A quick look at your astrology will reveal its duality of your sun sign, but on the reverse wheel where you resonate with the opposite sign, gradually the duality of your sun sign falls away. It is worth engaging with meditation and your spiritual development to rise above this duality you face on a daily basis. It is the conditioning of the mind that perpetuates duality. You may be of a fiery nature, but your opposite sign will, because of its energies coming into your expression, bring about a condition whereby the fiery nature does not create a negative cause and effect condition.

We also have to consider the duality of sun and moon. We know humanity started its descent into a physical being on Saturn, then the sun and then the moon. The moon chain came to an abrupt end, and now here we are in physical incarnation upon the earth governed by Karma (cause and effect, Saturn), and the sun and the moon, day and night, cycles and seasons. So, we have to consider the sun nature and the moon nature in relationship to our earthly existence. At the full moon, the sun is in alignment with the moon and the particular constellation it is aligned with, depending upon the time of year. Through that alignment, the spiritual energies come via the moon and so will have a great affect upon your consciousness. They could also have an unsettling affect upon your lower bodies if you are governed by them and seek to identify with the negative aspects of the alignment.

Remember, on the reverse wheel of astrology, the lower aspects fall away, so they are of no concern to you, but they will be for many. In a way, they can be a reason for the problems they are experiencing in the present, but the problem lies in the personality, not what is going on in the solar system and beyond. There is a sort of glamour concerning all this, yet there is some truth. How? Because of your integration with the soul, you are able to discriminate. Find your own truth, then find truth itself and through that, your purpose. Always, destiny calls you towards it. *'I let everything go to receive my purpose and destiny.'* Quite a statement of intent and remember, it is the Divine Will that gives you the resolve to continue towards your destiny. Nothing is ever lost upon that journey. You may think that you have left many things behind, but at some point, you will go full-circle although on a higher spiral, because at some point all this will happen, you won't have to think about it happening. You are on the path to destiny, and many things will occur, so expect the unexpected.

Become aware of your sun and moon natures, the light and the dark, activity and inactivity. There is a relationship here to the Fourth Ray of harmony – raja and tamas, activity and inactivity. You have to balance these two natures out within the self. Inactivity does not mean to do nothing, as most people understand that word, as there is the activity of the mind, the higher mind. The lower mind becomes inactive. Use the moon as a time for contemplation, for contacting your true nature, for the pondering of spiritual concepts, and for reading and writing. Create the time and space for this to happen – not when everything will allow you to do so. Do not be controlled by circumstance and give way to situations. You may not feel like doing these things as you are tired. This is a time for opportunity to overcome that which has caused you to be tired. Give that some thought. Your personality may be tired, but your soul is highly active, and remember, you have come a long way, so your soul will be more active than most, because you have set up a communication with your soul. The body may be tired, but your mind can still be active, and it matters not your age. The Hierarchy recognise your light (not your age), and your usefulness regarding the Divine Plan.

© Andrew Carter July 2023

Knowledge and Wisdom

There is no retirement from this endeavour. You are an intermediate between the Hierarchy and humanity. You are part of a group known as the *New Group of World Servers.* Many are part of this group and yet they are unknown to each other (all but those within your circle of influence), those who have the wisdom yet are quieter, until they are called upon to speak, then they have much to say, and you will find you also will have much to say. Have you noticed how much quieter you are with people who are not on the path? I don't mean that in a separatist way, it's just the way it is, because you have one foot in the lower words and the other in the higher worlds, and they may have both feet in the lower words, so their comments will be based upon that. The problem can lie when you are first dipping your toe, so to speak, in the higher worlds. There is a lot of apprehension in all that, and much uncertainty, as the higher worlds seem so nebulous and non-comprehensible.

What I have spoken about concerning the higher worlds cannot be proven, but the proof of the pudding is in the eating – one the sense of taste, the other the sense of touch. If you eventually put your foot into the higher worlds, then what is non-comprehensible becomes comprehensible through the results. This is happening to you, still you cannot prove the existence of those higher worlds, but what is said about them now becomes a reality, and you can then understand what, for example, an expanded consciousness means. It is the will that, when exercised, enables you to place your foot into the higher worlds. Let me bring in a relationship of your foot to your mind. What will you find there? To the lower mind, there will be nothing. The soul and the lower mind will form a triangle with the higher worlds, which are talked about as *dimensions.*

There is some very interesting talk about dimensions. I may be repeating myself with this, but it is important to understand the reality of thought concerning dimensions. We live in the third dimension and we cannot do otherwise about that physically, meaning our lower bodies. The only way is through the mind – this is the expansion of consciousness. People talk about accessing many dimensions above the soul, but if they had, then that would have an effect upon their consciousness. They would be enlightened to such an extent that they would lose their physical bodies and become Masters of the Wisdom or Masters of Compassion. But, has any change of consciousness happened to them in the light of the knowledge and wisdom you

© Andrew Carter July 2023

possess? You have, to a degree, integrated the soul into your consciousness, fourth dimension, and that has produced a transformation. You have dipped your toe.

If you can now engage in what is to follow:-

> Create a two-way flow between your mind and soul while focusing upon the periphery of time.
>
> On and off, your mind drifts beyond time. You are dipping your toe into the higher worlds. Drop into a state of nothing.
>
> Your mind is going beyond time, fully into the fourth dimensional divine mind, and touching the fifth, divine love.
>
> Stay within the state of nothing. There could be a communication, but have no expectation as that would drop you back into time and the lower worlds. Have a sense of discovery.

The important thing there was to achieve the state of nothing, and if that is all that happened, you would still have gone beyond time, although many would want to get something from that. There may have been a communication, but do not base your level of spiritual attainment upon whether you communicated or not. You see, when you are putting your foot into the higher worlds, you will be negating the astral plane. You have an understanding of the astral plane and its glamour related to the lower mental plane (illusion). In short, you will be cutting off the activity of the astral plane and its affects upon you, so there will be a void before the higher worlds imprint your consciousness. All these visions will go, unless, of course, they relate to a higher vision. People like to get something, and when they don't, they are unhappy. It's not the getting, it's the receiving. 'Getting' is for the self, 'receiving' is for the self *and* others. Always think that what you receive for yourself, you receive for others. This is a major key for receiving spiritual impression from the higher worlds. You have to adjust your thinking. Make that shift and you will see the difference.

© Andrew Carter July 2023

The Tibetan said that when he comes back, his main concern will be healing and etheric development. Everybody reading this book is a healer, and it is a very difficult task, healing others. Also retaining your status as a healer, meaning not allowing circumstance or environment to take you away from your purpose of healing, especially in this transition period. It is in this period that you are most needed, so call upon the will, when it is required, to renew your purpose. People may let you down and criticise you, and you may feel like giving up in the face of all this, but know you have our support, and healing others is a wonderful thing you are doing.

Your healings go far beyond the person you are healing, as through sensitivity of the problem they are suffering, the person you are healing will be identified with other people who have the same problem. They will not consciously know this. Just know that if you are healing one person, you could be healing many people. This is because you are working with energy of an etheric nature, and all things are connected upon an etheric level. You will be working multi-dimensionally, and breaking down the veils upon the astral and mental physical planes by the sheer fact you are bringing light through them, cutting a pathway through the receptivity of your triangle of head centres and your identification beyond them, into the spiritual planes and the source of healing. You will be bringing the energies onto the physical plane, so a healing is much more than you think it to be.

If healing is done in a group, and it doesn't have to be a large group, then the group becomes a powerful transmitter for healing energies. The power of identification creates an instant interlocking of energies between the group that is healing and those who they seek to heal, cutting a healing pathway through the etheric networks to the place of identification, and the group creates this by the use of the will and power of love, yet with the intelligence to know what you are doing.

The intuition can guide your healing without pre-empting any way of working. You have to be quite advanced to work in this way, and be impressed as to the methods and direction of the healing. You give over the direction of the healing to the intuition, which, in its truest sense, lives upon the Buddhic plane. With this method, it pays not to know the problem, as the logical mind, knowing the problem, will then work out the methods of healing with the knowledge it possesses. The intuition-will uses what knowledge you possess for directing the healing. It may come up with something new, but through all of this, you will still, after you have finished, know what you have done. You cannot say *'I was just guided. It wasn't me.'* That is absurd. You may also receive help for the healing - just know that will be happening. The intuition focuses upon the healing, not upon who may be helping you, or what energies are helping you. You will not speak about these things.

This presentation has now reached its conclusion. My hope is that you will benefit spiritually and personally from it. Always walk around with joy in your heart, and compassion for others. Invoke your will and purpose as you continue your journey towards your destiny.

Andrew Carter
27th August 2023

© Andrew Carter July 2023

Printed in Great Britain
by Amazon